Spanish
Essentials
FOR
DUMMIES®

**by Gail Stein, MA, and
Cecie Kraynak, MA**

WILEY

Wiley Publishing, Inc.

Spanish Essentials For Dummies®

Published by
Wiley Publishing, Inc.
111 River St.
Hoboken, NJ 07030-5774
www.wiley.com

For general information on our other products and services, please contact our Customer Care Department within the U.S. at 877-762-2974, outside the U.S. at 317-572-3993, or fax 317-572-4002.

For technical support, please visit www.wiley.com/techsupport.

Wiley also publishes its books in a variety of electronic formats. Some content that appears in print may not be available in electronic books.

Library of Congress Control Number: 2010924598

ISBN: 978-0-470-63751-7

Manufactured in the United States of America

10 9

WILEY

About the Authors

Gail Stein, MA, is a retired language instructor who taught in New York City public junior and senior high schools for more than 33 years. She has authored many French and Spanish books, including *CliffsQuickReview French I* and *II*, *CliffsStudySolver Spanish I* and *II*, *575+ French Verbs*, *Webster's Spanish Grammar Handbook,* and *Intermediate Spanish For Dummies*. Gail is a multiple-time honoree in *Who's Who Among America's Teachers*.

Cecie Kraynak, MA, earned her bachelor's degree in Spanish and secondary education in literature from Purdue University, and also received her master's degree in Spanish literature from Purdue. After graduating in 1983, Cecie began what was to become a 20-year career teaching Spanish to junior-high and high-school students. She continues to teach and travel and has served as a consultant on several Spanish learning guides, including *Teach Yourself Spanish in 24 Hours* (MacMillan) and *Spanish for Healthcare Professionals* (Barron's). She is the author of *Spanish Verbs For Dummies* (Wiley).

Publisher's Acknowledgments

We're proud of this book; please send us your comments at http://dummies.custhelp.com. For other comments, please contact our Customer Care Department within the U.S. at 877-762-2974, outside the U.S. at 317-572-3993, or fax 317-572-4002.

Some of the people who helped bring this book to market include the following:

Acquisitions, Editorial, and Media Development

Project Editor: Victoria M. Adang

Senior Acquisitions Editor: Lindsay Sandman Lefevere

Copy Editor: Megan Knoll

Assistant Editor: Erin Calligan Mooney

Senior Editorial Assistant: David Lutton

Technical Editors: Greg Harris; Language Training Center, Inc.

Editorial Manager: Michelle Hacker

Editorial Supervisor and Reprint Editor: Carmen Krikorian

Editorial Assistants: Rachelle Amick, Jennette ElNaggar

Cover Photo: © Corbis RF/Alamy

Cartoons: Rich Tennant (www.the5thwave.com)

Composition Services

Project Coordinator: Katie Crocker

Layout and Graphics: Claudia Bell, Carrie A. Cesavice, Christine Williams

Proofreaders: ConText Editorial Services, Inc., Rebecca Denoncour

Indexer: Potomac Indexing, LLC

Publishing and Editorial for Consumer Dummies

    Diane Graves Steele, Vice President and Publisher, Consumer Dummies

    Kristin Ferguson-Wagstaffe, Product Development Director, Consumer Dummies

    Ensley Eikenburg, Associate Publisher, Travel

    Kelly Regan, Editorial Director, Travel

Publishing for Technology Dummies

    Andy Cummings, Vice President and Publisher, Dummies Technology/General User

Composition Services

    Debbie Stailey, Director of Composition Services

Contents at a Glance

Contents

Introduction

● ●

*A*s someone who's studying Spanish, you want to write and speak correctly and to master the many different verb tenses and conjugations. *Spanish Essentials For Dummies* can help you reach your goals painlessly and effortlessly as you enhance your Spanish language skills.

Spanish Essentials For Dummies presents you with all the grammar you need to know to communicate clearly. With the help of this book, you'll be ready to have a conversation about topics besides your name and the weather! And that's something to be proud of.

About This Book

Spanish Essentials For Dummies is a reference book for people who have some knowledge of the fundamentals of Spanish. If you want to get up to speed with language structures so that you can communicate comfortably and proficiently, this book is for you.

Each chapter presents a different topic that allows you to practice your communication skills. We include plenty of examples to guide you through the rules so you're exposed to colloquial, everyday, correct Spanish that native speakers expect to hear from someone using Spanish. For example, the Spanish language has its individual idioms and idiomatic expressions that give it color and flair. Here's a quick example: To say that it's sunny outside in Spanish, you remark, **Hace sol.** The literal English translation of this expression is *It is making sun.* Even my dear old grandma wouldn't have spoken English like that! Well, make sure you don't speak Spanish that way, either.

Conventions Used in This Book

In order to highlight the most important information and to help you navigate this book more easily, we've set up several conventions:

- ✔ Spanish terms and sentences, as well as endings we want to highlight, are set in **boldface** to make them stand out.
- ✔ English equivalents, set in *italics*, follow the Spanish example.
- ✔ We use many abbreviations throughout the book. Don't let them throw you. For instance, you may find the following:
  - **fem.:** feminine
  - **masc.:** masculine
  - **sing.:** singular
  - **pl.:** plural

Foolish Assumptions

When writing this book, we made the following assumptions:

- ✔ You have some knowledge of the fundamentals of Spanish grammar. You're looking for the opportunity to review what you've already mastered and are intent on moving forward to new areas of knowledge.
- ✔ You want a book that's complete but isn't so advanced that you get lost in the rules. We try to explain the rules as clearly as possible without using too many grammatical terms.
- ✔ You're boning up on Spanish verbs for your own edification, or your son, daughter, grandson, granddaughter, niece, nephew, or special someone is studying Spanish and you want to help even though you haven't looked at a verb conjugation for years.

Icons Used in This Book

Icons are those cute little drawings on the left side of the page that call out for your attention. They signal a particularly valuable piece of information. Here's a list of the icons in this book:

Remember icons call your attention to important information about the language — something you shouldn't neglect or something that's out of the ordinary. Don't ignore these paragraphs.

 Tip icons present time-saving information that makes communication quick and effective. If you want to know the proper way to do things, check out the Tip icons first.

 The Warning icon points out certain differences between English and Spanish that you may find confusing. If you want to know how Spanish constructions differ from those in English, these are the paragraphs you need to consult.

Where to Go from Here

One great thing about *For Dummies* books is that you don't have to read them chapter by chapter from the very beginning to the (not-so) bitter end. Each chapter stands on its own and doesn't require that you complete any of the other chapters in the book. This setup saves you a lot of time if you've mastered certain topics but feel a bit insecure about others.

So, jump right in. Get your feet wet. If you're not sure exactly where to begin, take a good look at the table of contents and select the topic that seems to best fit your abilities and needs. If you're concerned that your background may not be strong enough, you can start at the very beginning and work your way through the book.

Keep in mind that studying Spanish isn't a contest. Work at a pace that best suits your needs. Don't hesitate to read a chapter a second, third, or even a fourth time several days later. You can easily adapt this book to your learning abilities. Remember, too, that you need to have a positive, confident attitude. Yes, you'll make mistakes. Everyone does — as a matter of fact, many native Spanish speakers do all the time. Your main goal should be to write and speak as well as you can; if you trip up and conjugate a verb incorrectly or use the feminine form of an adjective rather than the masculine form, it isn't the end of the world. If you can make yourself understood, you've won the greatest part of the battle.

The 5th Wave

By Rich Tennant

"Stop, stop, stop! I told you not to call a square dance in Spanish until you had the verbs down!"

Chapter 1

Brushing Up on the Basics

. . . .

In This Chapter

▶ Counting with cardinal and ordinal numbers

▶ Expressing dates

▶ Telling time

▶ Reviewing parts of speech

. . . .

Knowing numbers, expressing dates, relating the time of day, and recognizing parts of speech are essential Spanish skills you need in everyday life. Surely, the ability to communicate numbers, times, and dates is completely indispensable to you on a daily basis. Determining the correct part of speech to use helps you perfect your oral and written Spanish.

Counting Down

We start off this chapter with numbers because you need them in order to express dates and tell time. You use *cardinal numbers* (the more popular of the two) to count, to bargain with a merchant about a price, to express the temperature, or to write a check. You use *ordinal numbers* to express the number of a floor, the act of a play, or the order of a person in a race or competition.

Using cardinal numbers

You use cardinal numbers many times every day. As a matter of fact, you probably use them at least once an hour in the course of normal conversation or in writing. The Spanish cardinal numbers are as follows:

Number	Spanish	Number	Spanish
0	cero	25	veinticinco (veinte y cinco)
1	uno	26	veintiséis (veinte y seis)
2	dos	27	veintisiete (veinte y siete)
3	tres	28	veintiocho (veinte y ocho)
4	cuatro	29	veintinueve (veinte y nueve)
5	cinco	30	treinta
6	seis	40	cuarenta
7	siete	50	cincuenta
8	ocho	60	sesenta
9	nueve	70	setenta
10	diez	80	ochenta
11	once	90	noventa
12	doce	100	cien (ciento)
13	trece	101	ciento uno
14	catorce	200	doscientos
15	quince	500	quinientos
16	dieciséis (diez y seis)	700	setecientos
17	diecisiete (diez y siete)	900	novecientos
18	dieciocho (diez y ocho)	1.000	mil
19	diecinueve (diez y nueve)	2.000	dos mil
20	veinte	100.000	cien mil
21	veintiuno (veinte y uno)	1.000.000	un millón
22	veintidós (veinte y dos)	2.000.000	dos millones
23	veintitrés (veinte y tres)	1.000.000.000	mil millones
24	veinticuatro (veinte y cuatro)	2.000.000.000	dos mil millones

You need to keep the following rules in mind when using cardinal numbers in Spanish:

- ✔ **Uno** *(one)*, used only when counting, becomes **un** before a masculine noun and **una** before a feminine noun, whether the noun is singular or plural:

  - **uno, dos, tres** *(one, two, three)*
  - **un niño y una niña** *(a boy and a girl)*
  - **sesenta y un dólares** *(61 dollars)*
  - **veintiuna (veinte y una) personas** *(21 people)*

- ✔ You use the conjunction **y** *(and)* only for numbers between 16 and 99. You don't use it directly after hundreds:

  - **ochenta y ocho** *(88)*
  - **doscientos treinta y siete** *(237)*

- ✔ You generally write the numbers 16 through 19 and 21 through 29 as one word. The numbers 16, 22, 23, and 26 have accents on the last syllable:

  - 16: **dieciséis**
  - 22: **veintidós**
  - 23: **veintitrés**
  - 26: **veintiséis**

- ✔ When used before a masculine noun, **veintiún** *(21)* has an accent on the last syllable:

  - **veintiún días** *(21 days)*

- ✔ **Ciento** *(100)* becomes **cien** before nouns of either gender and before the numbers **mil** and **millones**. Before all other numbers, you use **ciento**. **Un** *(one)*, which you don't use before **cien(to)** or **mil**, comes before **millón**. When a noun follows **millón**, you put the preposition **de** between **millón** and the noun. **Millón** drops its accent in the plural **(millones)**:

  - **cien sombreros** *(100 hats)*
  - **cien blusas** *(100 blouses)*
  - **cien mil millas** *(100,000 miles)*
  - **cien millones de dólares** *(100 million dollars)*

- **ciento noventa acres** *(190 acres)*
- **mil posibilidades** *(1,000 possibilities)*
- **un millón de razones** *(1 million reasons)*

✔ Compounds of **ciento (doscientos, trescientos)** must change to agree with a feminine noun:

- **cuatrocientos muchachos** *(400 muchachos)*
- **seiscientas muchachas** *(600 muchachas)*

With numerals and decimals, Spanish uses commas where English uses periods, and vice versa:

English	Spanish
6,000	6.000
0.75	0,75
$14.99	$14,99

Using ordinal numbers

You use *ordinal numbers* — those used to express numbers in a series — far less frequently than cardinal numbers, but they still have some very important applications in everyday life. The following chart presents the Spanish ordinal numbers:

Ordinal	Spanish
1st	**primero**
2nd	**segundo**
3rd	**tercero**
4th	**cuarto**
5th	**quinto**
6th	**sexto**
7th	**séptimo**
8th	**octavo**
9th	**noveno**
10th	**décimo**

The following list outlines everything you must remember when using ordinal numbers in Spanish:

- Spanish speakers rarely use ordinal numbers after 10th. After that, they usually use cardinal numbers in both the spoken and written language:

  El siglo quince *(the 15th century)*

- Ordinal numbers must agree in gender (masculine or feminine) with the nouns they modify. You can make ordinal numbers feminine by changing the final **-o** of the masculine form to **-a**:

  la cuarta vez *(the fourth time)*

- **Primero** and **tercero** drop the final **-o** before a masculine singular noun:

  el primer muchacho *(the first boy)*

  el tercer hombre *(the third man)*

- In dates, **primero** is the only ordinal number you use. All other dates call for the cardinal numbers:

  el primero de mayo *(May 1st)*

  el doce de enero *(January 12th)*

Dealing with Dates

Dates are important parts of everyday life (in more ways than one!). To write out dates in Spanish, you have to practice the days of the week, the months of the year, and numbers (see the preceding section).

Expressing the days of the week

If you hear **¿Qué día es hoy?** *(What day is it?),* you should respond with **Hoy es . . .** *(Today is . . .)* and then provide the name of one of the days listed here:

English	Spanish
Monday	**lunes**
Tuesday	**martes**
Wednesday	**miércoles**
Thursday	**jueves**
Friday	**viernes**
Saturday	**sábado**
Sunday	**domingo**

Unlike the English calendar, the Spanish calendar starts with Monday.

Here are two more guidelines for talking about days of the week in Spanish:

- ✔ Unless you use them at the beginning of a sentence, you don't capitalize the days of the week in Spanish:

  Lunes y martes son días de vacaciones. *(Monday and Tuesday are vacation days.)*

- ✔ You use **el** to express *on* when referring to a particular day of the week and **los** to express *on* when the action occurs repeatedly:

  No trabajo el sábado. *(I'm not working on Saturday.)*

  No trabajo los sábados. *(I don't work on Saturdays.)*

Naming the months of the year

If you hear ¿**En qué mes . . .?** *(In what month . . .)*, someone is asking you in what month a certain event takes place. We provide the names of the months in Spanish in the following list:

English	Spanish
January	**enero**
February	**febrero**
March	**marzo**
April	**abril**
May	**mayo**
June	**junio**
July	**julio**
August	**agosto**
September	**septiembre (or setiembre)**
October	**octubre**
November	**noviembre**
December	**diciembre**

Like days of the week, the months aren't capitalized in Spanish:

> **Junio y julio son meses agradables.** *(June and July are nice months.)*

Along with the months, you may also want to talk about the seasons of the year. In Spanish, the seasons are masculine except for **la primavera** *(the spring):*

> **el invierno** *(the winter)*
>
> **la primavera** *(the spring)*
>
> **el verano** *(the summer)*
>
> **el otoño** *(the autumn [fall])*

Making a date

If you want to ask a passerby or an acquaintance about the date, politely inquire **¿Cuál es la fecha de hoy?** *(What is today's date?)* The person should respond with **Hoy es . . .** *(Today is . . .)* and then use the following formula to express the correct date:

> day + **(el)** + cardinal number (except for **primero**) + **de** + month + **de** + year

The following is an example translation, using this formula:

> *Sunday, April 18, 2010:* **Hoy es domingo, el dieciocho de abril de dos mil diez.**

Now that you have a handy formula, you need to know a few more details about writing dates in Spanish:

✔ You express the first day of each month with **primero.** You use cardinal numbers for all other days:

el primero de enero *(January 1st)*

el siete de enero *(January 7th)*

✔ Use **el** to express *on* with Spanish dates:

Partimos el once de octubre. *(We are leaving on October 11th.)*

> ✔ In Spanish, you express years in thousands and hundreds, not only in hundreds:
>
> *1492:* **mil cuatrocientos noventa y dos** *(fourteen hundred ninety-two)*

In Spanish, when dates are written as numbers, they follow the sequence day/month/year, which may prove confusing to English speakers — especially for dates below the 12th of the month. You write *February 9th* as 2/9 in English, but in Spanish it's 9/2.

When speaking of dates in everyday language, the words and expressions that follow may come in handy:

English	Spanish	English	Spanish
a day	**un día**	*day before yesterday*	**anteayer**
a week	**una semana**	*yesterday*	**ayer**
a month	**un mes**	*today*	**hoy**
a year	**un año**	*tomorrow*	**mañana**
in	**en**	*tomorrow morning*	**mañana por la mañana**
ago	**hace**	*tomorrow afternoon*	**mañana por la tarde**
per	**por**	*tomorrow night*	**mañana por la noche**
during	**durante**	*day after tomorrow*	**pasado mañana**
next	**próximo(a)**	*from*	**desde**
last	**pasado(a)**	*a week from today*	**de hoy en ocho**
last (in a series)	**último(a)**	*two weeks from tomorrow*	**de mañana en dos semanas**
eve	**la víspera**	*within one (two) week(s)*	**dentro de una (dos) semana(s)**

Telling Time

Knowing how to understand, speak, and write time-related words and phrases is a must for anyone who's studying a foreign language and planning to put these studies to use (to do some traveling one day, for instance).

If you hear **¿Qué hora es?** *(What time is it?)*, someone wants to know the time. You should start by responding with the following:

> **Es la una** + 1 o'clock hour or **Son las** + any time after 1.

To express the time after the hour (up to and including half past the hour), use **y** *(and)* and the number of minutes. Use **menos** *(less)* + the number of the following hour to express the time before the next hour (after half past the hour).

You can also express time numerically (as shown in the third example here):

> **Es la una y media.** *(It's 1:30.)*
>
> **Son las cinco menos veinte.** *(It's 4:40.)*
>
> **Son las cuatro y cuarenta.** *(It's 4:40.)*

If you want to discuss at what time a particular event will occur, you can use a question — **¿A qué hora . . . ?** — or answer with **A la una** or **A las** + any time after 1:

> **¿A qué hora vienen?** *(At what time are they coming?)*
>
> **A la una.** *(At 1:00.)*
>
> **A las tres y cuarto.** *(At 3:15.)*

The following chart shows how to express time after and before the hour:

Time	*Spanish*
1:00	**la una**
2:05	**las dos y cinco**
3:10	**las tres y diez**
4:15	**las cuatro y cuarto** or **las cuatro y quince**
5:20	**las cinco y veinte**
6:25	**las seis y veinticinco**
7:30	**las siete y media** or **las siete y treinta**
7:35	**las ocho menos veinticinco** or **las siete y treinta y cinco**
8:40	**las nueve menos veinte** or **las ocho y cuarenta**
9:45	**las diez menos cuarto** or **las nueve y cuarenta y cinco**

Time	Spanish
10:50	**las once menos diez** or **las diez y cincuenta**
11:55	**las doce menos cinco** or **las once y cincuenta y cinco**
noon	**el mediodía**
midnight	**la medianoche**

When expressing time, the words and expressions we present in the following table may come in handy:

English	Spanish	English	Spanish
a second	**un segundo**	in an hour	**en una hora**
a minute	**un minuto**	in a while	**dentro de un rato**
a quarter of an hour	**un cuarto de hora**	until ten o'clock	**hasta las diez**
an hour	**una hora**	before nine o'clock	**antes de las nueve**
a half hour	**media hora**	after seven o'clock	**después de las siete**
in the morning (a.m.)	**por la mañana**	since what time?	**¿desde qué hora?**
in the afternoon (p.m.)	**por la tarde**	since eight o'clock	**desde las ocho**
in the evening (p.m.)	**por la noche**	one hour ago	**hace una hora**
at what time?	**¿a qué hora?**	early	**temprano**
at exactly nine o'clock	**a las nueve en punto**	late	**tarde**
at about two o'clock	**a eso de las dos**	late (in arriving)	**de retraso**

Focusing on Parts of Speech

Too many people try to translate word for word from English to Spanish. And that just doesn't work. Why? Because a Spanish word may have many applications depending on its usage (for example, as a noun or as an adjective) in the sentence. In addition, many idiomatic phrases, when used properly, distinguish a native speaker from someone who's unfamiliar with the language. (An *idiomatic* phrase is a phrase used in a particular language whose meaning can't easily be understood by a literal translation of its component words. An English example is "It's raining cats and dogs.")

Using nouns

A *noun* is the part of speech that refers to a person, place, thing, quality, idea, or action. Here are some examples of nouns in action:

- Person: *The <u>boy</u> is friendly.* (**El <u>muchacho</u> es amable.**)
- Place: *I want to go <u>home</u>.* (**Quiero ir a <u>casa</u>.**)
- Thing: *I would like to see that <u>book</u>.* (**Quisiera ver ese <u>libro</u>.**)
- Quality: *I admire her <u>courage</u>.* (**Admiro su <u>coraje</u>.**)
- Idea: *<u>Communism</u> is a political theory.* (**El <u>comunismo</u> es una teoría política.**)
- Action: *The plane's <u>departure</u> is imminent.* (**La <u>partida</u> del avión es inminente.**)

In everyday speaking/writing, you use nouns most often in the following forms:

- As the subject of a verb:

  <u>María</u> speaks Spanish. (**<u>María</u> habla español.**)
- As the direct object of a verb:

  I see <u>María</u>. (**Yo veo a <u>María</u>.**)
- As the indirect object of a verb:

  I speak to <u>María</u>. (**Yo le hablo a <u>María</u>.**)
- As the object of a preposition:

  I went out with María. (**Yo salí con <u>María</u>.**)

Unlike English nouns, all Spanish nouns have a gender: masculine or feminine. All words you use to qualify or describe a noun must agree with the noun with respect to gender. We discuss this in more detail in Chapter 2.

Substituting pronouns

A *pronoun* is a part of speech used in place of a noun. The following list outlines the pronouns we discuss in this book:

- ✔ *Subject pronouns* (see Chapter 3) are followed by the verb expressing the main action in the sentence *(I, you, he, she, it, we, they)*:

  <u>You</u> *are nice.* (**<u>Ud.</u> es simpático.**)

- ✔ *Interrogative pronouns* (see Chapter 5) ask a question *(who, which, what,* and so on):

  <u>Who</u> *is that?* (**¿<u>Quién</u> es?**)

- ✔ *Direct object pronouns* (see Chapter 2) replace direct object nouns; they answer whom or what the subject is acting upon. The direct object pronouns are **me, te, lo, la** (**le** in Spain), **nos,** (**os** in Spain), **los,** and **las** (**les** in Spain):

  I'll be seeing <u>you</u>. (**<u>Te</u> veo.**)

- ✔ *Indirect object pronouns* (see Chapter 2) replace indirect object nouns; they explain to or for whom something is done. They include **me, te, le, nos,** (**os** in Spain), and **les:**

  He wrote to <u>me</u>. (**<u>Me</u> escribió.**)

- ✔ *Reflexive pronouns* (see Chapter 3) show that the subject is acting upon itself (**me, te, se, nos,** [**os** in Spain]):

  He sees <u>himself</u> in the mirror. (**Él <u>se</u> ve en el espejo.**)

- ✔ *Prepositional pronouns* (see Chapter 4) are used after prepositions (**mí, ti, él, ella, Ud., nosotros, vosotros** (in Spain), **ellos, ellas, Uds.**):

  They're going to the movies without <u>me</u>. (**Van al cine sin <u>mí</u>.**)

Acting with verbs

A verb is a part of speech that shows an action or a state of being. In Spanish, as in English, verbs change from their infinitive form (they're conjugated, in other words) as follows:

- ✔ To agree with the person performing the action (I, you, he, she, it, we, they)

✔ To indicate the time when the action was performed (past, present, future)

✔ To indicate the mood (indicative, subjunctive, imperative, conditional) of the action

The *infinitive* of the verb is its "raw" form — its "to" form — before it's conjugated. Infinitives in Spanish have three different endings, and you conjugate them according to these endings (**-ar, -er,** and **-ir**) when a subject is present or is implied. We give you lots more information about verbs in Chapters 3, 6, 7, and 8.

Describing with adjectives

An *adjective* is a part of speech that describes a noun:

> The house is <u>white</u>. (**La casa es <u>blanca</u>.**)

A Spanish adjective can have other applications, too, which we outline in the following list:

✔ A *possessive adjective* tells to whom the noun belongs:

> It's <u>my</u> book. (**Es <u>mi</u> libro.**)

✔ A *demonstrative adjective* shows *this, that, these,* or *those:*

> <u>That</u> film is good. (**<u>Esa</u> película es buena.**)

✔ An *interrogative adjective* asks the question *whose, which,* or *what:*

> <u>Whose</u> car is that? (**<u>¿De quién</u> es ese coche?**)

✔ A number (cardinal or ordinal; see the "Counting Down" section earlier in this chapter) is an adjective that gives a specific amount:

> I need <u>a</u> pen. (**Necesito <u>un</u> bolígrafo.**)

> It's his <u>tenth</u> birthday. (**Es su <u>décimo</u> cumpleaños.**)

Clarifying with adverbs

An *adverb* is a part of speech that modifies a verb, an adjective, or another adverb:

 ✔ Modifying a verb: *You speak quickly.* **(Ud. habla rápidamente.)**

 ✔ Modifying an adjective: *Her grandmother is very old.* **(Su abuela es muy vieja.)**

 ✔ Modifying an adverb: *They eat too slowly.* **(Ellos comen demasiado despacio.)**

Joining with prepositions

Prepositions are words used before nouns or pronouns to relate them to other words in the sentence. Prepositions connect the following:

 ✔ Noun to noun: *I need that piece of paper.* **(Necesito esa hoja de papel.)**

 ✔ Verb to verb: *The child begins to laugh.* **(El niño empieza a reír.)**

 ✔ Verb to noun: *She studies with her friends.* **(Ella estudia con sus amigas.)**

 ✔ Verb to pronoun: *What do you think about them?* **(¿Qué piensas de ellos?)**

Chapter 2

Closing the Gender Gap

. . . .

. . . .

*L*et the battle of the sexes begin! Gender is a battle that English speakers don't fight. In English, a noun is simply a noun; you don't have to worry about a noun having a gender (a masculine or feminine designation). In Spanish, however, a noun has a gender, and the gender of a noun very often determines the spelling of other words in the sentence.

In this chapter, we help you to correctly mark the gender of a noun by using definite articles (which express *the*), indefinite articles (which express *a, an,* or *some*), or demonstrative adjectives (which express *this, that, these,* or *those*). You can also read up on two different ways to show possession of things and how to replace direct and indirect object nouns with their respective pronouns.

Being Specific with Definite Articles

A *definite article* expresses the English word *the* and indicates a specific person or thing, such as "the boy" or "the book."

You must choose the correct definite article to "mark" a noun in order to say *the*.

Identifying the definite articles

Spanish features four distinct definite articles that correspond to *the* in English. The following table lists these articles:

	Masculine	*Feminine*
Singular	**el**	**la**
Plural	**los**	**las**

Here are some examples of these definitive articles in action:

El muchacho es grande. *(The boy is big.)*

Los libros son interesantes. *(The books are interesting.)*

La muchacha es alta. *(The girl is tall.)*

Las casas son blancas. *(The houses are white.)*

Using definite articles

You come across many instances in Spanish where you use the definite article even though you may or may not use it in English. The rules in the following list show how you use the definite articles in Spanish:

✔ With nouns in a general or abstract sense:

  • **El amor es divino.** *(Love is divine.)*

✔ With nouns in a specific sense:

  • **La tía María trae regalos.** *(Aunt María brings gifts.)*

✔ With names of languages (except after the verb **hablar** and after the prepositions **de** and **en**):

  • **Me gusta el español.** *(I like Spanish.)*

  • **¿Dónde está mi libro de español?** *(Where's my Spanish book?)*

  • **Escríbame en español.** *(Write to me in Spanish.)*

✔ With parts of the body (when the possessor is clear) in place of the possessive adjective:

- **Me duelen los pies.** *(My feet hurt.)*

✔ With titles and ranks when you aren't addressing the person:

- **La señora Rivera está aquí.** *(Mrs. Rivera is here.)*
- **Siéntese, Señora Rivera.** *(Have a seat, Mrs. Rivera.)*

✔ With last names:

- **Los Gómez viven en Colombia.** *(The Gómezes live in Colombia.)*

✔ With days of the week (except after the verb **ser**):

- **El domingo voy a México.** *(On Sunday I'm going to Mexico.)*
- **Hoy es miércoles.** *(*Today is Wednesday.*)*

✔ With seasons (you may omit the article after **en**):

- **No trabajo en (el) verano.** *(I don't work in the summer.)*

✔ With dates:

- **Es el cinco de mayo.** *(It's May 5th.)*

✔ With the hour of the day and other time expressions:

- **Son las once y media.** *(It's 11:30.)*
- **Salgo por la tarde.** *(I'm going out in the afternoon.)*

✔ With the names of many cities and countries (though there's a tendency to omit the article in current usage):

- **el Brasil, el Ecuador, El Escorial, el Paraguay, el Perú, El Salvador, el Uruguay, la Argentina, la China, La Habana, la India, La Paz, los Estados Unidos**
- **Visitamos (el) Brasil.** *(We visited Brazil.)*

Capitalized articles are actually parts of the names of the countries, whereas articles in lowercase are not. For example, **Yo nací en El Salvador pero pasé muchos años en la Argentina.** *(I was born in El Salvador but I spent many years in Argentina.)*

✔ With rivers, seas, and other geographical locations:

• **El Orinoco es un río.** *(The Orinoco is a river.)*

The definite article precedes the noun it modifies and agrees with that noun in number and gender. For example, **El muchacho es rubio y las muchachas son morenas.** *(The boy is blond and the girls are brunette.)*

Omitting the definite articles

You omit the definite articles in the following situations in Spanish:

✔ Before nouns in *apposition* (when one noun explains another):

Madrid, capital de España, es una ciudad popular. *(Madrid, the capital of Spain, is a popular city.)*

✔ Before numerals that express the title of rulers:

Carlos Quinto *(Charles the Fifth)*

Contracting with definite articles

Spanish features only two contractions. They occur when the definite article el is joined with the preposition **a (a** + **el** = **al)** or **de (de** + **el** = **del).** The only exception to the rule is when the definite article is part of the title or name. Here are some examples of this construction:

Voy al Uruguay. *(I'm going to Uruguay.)* **Voy a El Salvador.** *(I'm going to El Salvador.)*

Soy del Uruguay. *(I'm from Uruguay.)* **Soy de El Salvador.** *(I'm from El Salvador.)*

Being General with Indefinite Articles

An *indefinite article,* which expresses the English words *a, an,* or *some,* refers to persons or objects not specifically identified (such as "a boy" or "some books"). Just like with definite articles, when you know whether a noun is masculine or feminine (and singular or plural), you can choose the correct indefinite article to mark that noun.

Identifying the indefinite articles

Four Spanish indefinite articles correspond to *a, an,* and *one* in the singular and to *some* in the plural. The following table presents these articles:

	Masculine	**Feminine**
Singular	**un**	**una**
Plural	**unos**	**unas**

Here are some examples of the indefinite articles in action:

> **Compré un abrigo.** *(She bought an [one] overcoat.)*
>
> **Es una mujer muy astuta.** *(She is a very astute woman.)*
>
> **Necesito unos limones y unas limas.** *(I need some lemons and some limes.)*

As with definite articles, the indefinite article precedes the noun it modifies and agrees with that noun in number and gender.

Omitting indefinite articles

You omit the indefinite article from your Spanish constructions in the following situations:

> ✔ Before unmodified nouns that express nationality, profession, or religious or political affiliation:
>
> > • **El señor Robles es profesor.** *(Mr. Robles is a teacher.)*
>
> However, you use the indefinite article when the noun is modified:
>
> > • **El señor Robles es un profesor liberal.** *(Mr. Robles is a liberal teacher.)*

✔ Before the following nouns:

- **cien** *(one hundred):* **cien niños** *(one hundred children)*
- **cierto** *(certain):* **ciertos idiomas** *(certain languages)*
- **mil** *(one thousand):* **mil dólares** *(one thousand dollars)*
- **otro** *(other):* **otra clase** *(another class)*
- **qué** *(what a):* **qué lástima** *(what a pity)*
- **semejante** *(similar):* **problema semejante** *(a similar problem)*
- **tal** *(such a):* **tal cosa** *(such a thing)*

Being Demonstrative with Adjectives

Personally, we're not content with just anything or anyone; we like to make our requirements and needs known! We do so by specifically referring to *this, that, these,* or *those* things or people. If you're like us, you need to make use of the Spanish demonstrative adjectives that enable you to express exactly what or whom you're seeking.

Demonstrative adjectives indicate or point out the person, place, or thing to which a speaker is referring, such as "this shirt" or "that pair of pants." Demonstrative adjectives precede and agree in number and gender with the nouns they modify. In Spanish, you select the demonstrative adjective according to the distance of the noun from the speaker. Table 2-1 presents demonstrative adjectives and addresses this distance issue.

Table 2-1	Demonstrative Adjectives			
Number	*Masculine*	*Feminine*	*Meaning*	*Distance*
Singular	**este**	**esta**	*this*	Near to or directly concerned with speaker
Plural	**estos**	**estas**	*these*	

Number	Masculine	Feminine	Meaning	Distance
Singular	ese	esa	*that*	Not particularly
Plural	esos	esas	*those*	near to or directly
				concerned with
				speaker
Singular	aquel	aquella	*that*	Far from and not
Plural	aquellos	aquellas	*those*	directly concerned
				with speaker

The following list shows these demonstrative adjectives in action:

> **Estos pantalones son cortos y esta camisa es larga.**
> *(These pants are short and this shirt is large.)*

> **Tengo que hablar con esa muchacha y esos muchachos ahí.** *(I have to speak to that girl and those boys there.)*

> **Aquellos países son grandes y aquellas ciudades son pequeñas.** *(Those countries are large and those cities are small.)*

Here's what you need to know about demonstrative adjectives in Spanish:

✔ You use them before each noun:

- **este abogado y ese cliente** *(this lawyer and that client)*

✔ You can use adverbs to reinforce location:

- **esta casa aquí** *(this house here)*
- **esas casas ahí** *(those houses there)*
- **aquella casa allá** *(that house over there)*

Clarifying Gender

Spanish nouns are either masculine or feminine. Nouns that refer to males are always masculine, and nouns that refer to females are feminine, no matter their endings. You can't always be sure when it comes to places or things, though.

Determining the gender of nouns

In Spanish, certain endings are good indications as to the *gender* (masculine or feminine designation) of nouns. For instance, nouns that end in **-o** (except **la mano** *[the hand]* and **la radio** *[the radio]*) often are masculine. Nouns that end in **-a, -ad** (**la ciudad** *[city]*), **-ie** (**la serie** *[the series]*), **-ción** (**la canción** *[the song]*), **-sión** (**la discusión** *[discussion]*), **-ud** (**la salud** *[health]*), and **-umbre** (**la costumbre** *[custom]*) generally are feminine.

Here are more rules that deal with gender in Spanish:

- Certain nouns belonging to a theme are masculine. These include

  - Numbers: **el cuatro** *(four)*
  - Days of the week: **el jueves** *(Thursday)*
  - Compass points: **el norte** *(north)*
  - Names of trees: **el manzano** *(apple tree)*
  - Some compound nouns: **el sacapuntas** *(pencil sharpener)*
  - Names of rivers, lakes, mountains, straits, and seas: **el Mediterráneo** *(the Mediterranean)*

- Certain nouns belonging to a theme are feminine. These include

  - Many illnesses: **la gripe** *(the flu)*, **la apendicitis** *(appendicitis)*
  - Islands and provinces: **la Córsega** *(Corsica)*

Reversing gender

Some Spanish nouns are tricky because they end in **-a** but are masculine, while others end in **-o** but are feminine. These nouns may be referred to as *reverse-gender nouns.* For instance, some nouns that end in **-ma** and **-eta** are masculine, as are the words **el día** *(the day)* and **el mapa** *(the map).* The following table outlines these masculine words:

-ma	*-eta*
el clima *(the climate)*	**el planeta** *(the planet)*
el drama *(the drama)*	
el idioma *(the language)*	
el poema *(the poem)*	
el problema *(the problem)*	
el programa *(the program)*	
el sistema *(the system)*	
el telegrama *(the telegram)*	
el tema *(the theme)*	

Here are a couple of nouns that end in **-o** and are feminine:

- ✔ **la mano** *(the hand)*
- ✔ **la radio** *(the radio)*

Note that **la foto** is the abbreviation for **la fotografía** *(the photograph)* and **la moto** is the abbreviation for **la motocicleta** *(the motorcycle)*.

Using the same noun for both genders

Some nouns have the same spelling for both genders. For these nouns, all you have to do is change the definite article to reflect whether the person in question is male or female. The following table presents the most common of these nouns:

Masculine	*Feminine*	*Translation*
el artista	**la artista**	*the artist*
el dentista	**la dentista**	*the dentist*
el periodista	**la periodista**	*the journalist*
el telefonista	**la telefonista**	*the operator*
el modelo	**la modelo**	*the model*
el joven	**la joven**	*the youth*
el estudiante	**la estudiante**	*the student*

The following nouns, however, always remain feminine, regardless of the gender of the person being described:

✔ **la persona** *(the person)*

✔ **la víctima** *(the victim)*

Changing the meaning of nouns

Some nouns change meaning according to their gender. A noun in this category can mean one thing in the masculine form but have a totally different meaning in the feminine form. Knowing the proper usage is the difference between praying to the Pope or to a potato! You simply must memorize nouns in this category. The following table presents some of the high-frequency Spanish words whose meanings change according to gender:

Masculine	Meaning	Feminine	Meaning
el capital	the capital (money)	la capital	the capital (country)
el cura	the priest	la cura	the cure
el frente	the front	la frente	the forehead
el guía	the male guide	la guía	the female guide; the guidebook
el Papa	the Pope	la papa	the potato
el policía	the police officer	la policía	the police force; the police woman

Understanding special nouns

When it comes to languages, you can always find some exceptions to the rule. In Spanish, for instance, masculine nouns that refer to people and end in **-or, -és,** or **-n** require the addition of a final **-a** to get the female equivalent. And if the masculine noun has an accented final syllable, you drop that accent in the feminine form. Here are some examples:

el profesor → **la profesora** *(the teacher)*

el francés → **la francesa** *(the French person)*

el alemán → **la alemana** *(the German person)*

Of course, you must watch out for two exceptions to this rule:

- ✔ **el actor** *(the actor)* → **la actriz** *(the actress)*
- ✔ **el emperador** *(the emperor)* → **la emperatriz** *(the empress)*

Some nouns have distinct masculine and feminine forms. The following table presents a list of these nouns, which you simply have to memorize:

Masculine	*Meaning*	*Feminine*	*Meaning*
el héroe	*the hero*	**la heroína**	*the heroine*
el hombre	*the man*	**la mujer**	*the woman*
el marido	*the husband*	**la esposa**	*the wife*
el príncipe	*the prince*	**la princesa**	*the princess*
el rey	*the king*	**la reina**	*the queen*
el yerno	*the son-in-law*	**la nuera**	*the daughter-in-law*

To prevent the clash of two vowel sounds, the Spanish language uses the masculine singular article **el (un)** with feminine singular nouns that begin with a stressed *a* sound **(a-** or **ha-).** In the plural, you use **las (unas)** for these nouns. Here are some commonly used words with this designation:

el agua *(the water);* **las aguas** *(the waters)*

el ave *(the bird);* **las aves** *(the birds)*

el hambre *(the hunger);* **las hambres** *(the hungers)*

Forming Plural Nouns

You use *noun plurals* to refer to more than one person, place, thing, quality, idea, or action. Not surprisingly, just as you do in English, you use the letters **-s** and **-es** to form the plurals of Spanish nouns. The following list outlines the many plural variations you see in Spanish nouns and the rules for forming plurals:

- ✔ You add **-s** to form the plural of nouns ending in a vowel:
  - **el mango** *(the mango);* **los mangos** *(the mangoes)*
  - **la manzana** *(the apple);* **las manzanas** *(the apples)*

✔ You add **-es** to form the plural of nouns ending in a consonant (including **-y**):

- **el emperador** *(the emperor);* **los emperadores** *(the emperors)*
- **el rey** *(the king);* **los reyes** *(the kings)*

✔ You add or delete an accent mark in some nouns ending in **-n** or **-s** to maintain the original stress:

- **el examen; los exámenes** *(the tests)*
- **la canción; las canciones** *(the songs)*
- **el francés; los franceses** *(the Frenchmen)*
- **el inglés; los ingleses** *(the Englishmen)*
- **el limón; los limones** *(the lemons)*

✔ Nouns that end in **-z** change **z** to **-c** before you add **-es:**

- **la luz** *(the light);* **las luces** *(the lights)*

✔ Nouns that end in **-es** or **-is** don't change in the plural, except for **el mes** *(the month),* which becomes **los meses** *(the months):*

- **el lunes** *(Monday);* **los lunes** *(Mondays)*
- **la crisis** *(the crisis);* **las crisis** *(the crises)*

✔ Compound nouns (nouns composed of two nouns that join together to make one) don't change in the plural:

- **el abrelatas** (can opener); **los abrelatas** (can openers)

✔ You express the plural of nouns of different genders (where one noun is masculine and the other[s] is feminine) with the masculine plural:

- **el rey y la reina** *(the king and queen);* **los reyes** *(the kings or the king[s] and the queen[s])*
- **el muchacho y la muchacha** *(the boy and the girl);* **los muchachos** *(the boys or the boy[s] and the girl[s])*

✔ Some nouns are always plural, such as

- **las gafas/los espejuelos** *(eyeglasses)*
- **las matemáticas** *(mathematics)*
- **las vacaciones** *(vacation)*

Showing Possession

The majority of people in the world are possessive of their loved ones and their things. You have several ways to express possession in Spanish: by using the preposition **de** *(of)* or by using possessive adjectives before the persons or things. The sections that follow guide you through the ways you can stake your claims.

Using de

Expressing possession by using the preposition **de** *(of)* is quite unlike what people are accustomed to in English. English speakers put an apostrophe + *s* after the noun representing the possessor: John's family, for instance. Spanish nouns have no apostrophe *s;* you must use a reverse word order joined by the preposition **de.** The following list presents the rules of using **de:**

✔ You use the preposition **de** between a noun that's possessed and a proper noun representing the possessor:

Es el coche de Julio. *(It's Julio's car.)*

✔ You use **de** + a definite article between the noun that's possessed and a common noun representing the possessor:

Tengo el abrigo de la muchacha. *(I have the girl's coat.)*

✔ **De** contracts with the definite article **el** to form **del** *(of the)* before a masculine singular common noun:

Necesito el libro del profesor. *(I need the teacher's book.)*

✔ If the sentence contains more than one possessor, you need to repeat **de** before each noun:

Voy a la casa de Roberto y de Marta. *(I'm going to Roberto and Marta's house.)*

✔ You use a construction that's the reverse of English to answer the question "**¿De quién es . . .?**":

¿De quién(es) es la idea? *(Whose idea is it?)*

Es la idea de Julia y del hermano de Julia. *(It is Julia's and her brother's idea.)*

Employing possessive adjectives

You use a *possessive adjective* before the noun that's possessed in order to express *my, your, his, her, its, our,* or *their.* Possessive adjectives must agree in gender and number (singular or plural) with the objects that are possessed; they never agree with the possessors. Table 2-2 outlines the possessive adjectives:

Table 2-2	Possessive Adjectives			
English word	*Masculine singular*	*Masculine plural*	*Feminine singular*	*Feminine plural*
my	**mi**	**mis**	**mi**	**mis**
your	**tu**	**tus**	**tu**	**tus**
his/her/your	**su**	**sus**	**su**	**sus**
our	**nuestro**	**nuestros**	**nuestra**	**nuestras**
your	**vuestro**	**vuestros**	**vuestra**	**vuestras**
their/your	**su**	**sus**	**su**	**sus**

Here are some example sentences:

> **Yo perdí mis gafas.** *(I lost my glasses.)*

> **Nosotros escuchamos a nuestro profesor.** *(We listen to our teacher.)*

Because **su** can mean *his, her,* or *their,* you can clarify who the possessor really is by replacing the possessive adjective **(su)** with the corresponding definite article **(el, la, los, or las)** + noun + **de** + **él (ellos, ella, ellas, Ud., Uds.):**

> *I need his (her) help.*

> **Necesito su ayuda.**

> **Necesito la ayuda de él (ella).**

With parts of the body or clothing, you replace the possessive adjective with the correct definite article when the possessor is clear:

> **Me cepillo los dientes dos veces al día.** *(I brush my teeth twice a day.)*

Substituting with Object Pronouns

An object pronoun is a replacement word for an object noun. This pronoun helps you avoid unnecessary, continuous repetition of the noun, which allows for a more colloquial, free-flowing conversational tone when you're speaking or writing. Don't be tricked by these pronouns, though; always remember that the verb in your sentence must agree with the subject pronoun. The following sections walk you through the world of object pronouns.

Dealing with direct object pronouns

Direct object nouns or *pronouns* answer the question "Whom or what is the subject acting upon?" Direct objects may refer to people, places, things, or ideas. A direct object pronoun simply replaces a direct object noun and agrees with it in number and gender.

In both English and Spanish, a direct object noun follows the subject and its verb:

Veo la casa. *(I see the house.)*

Unlike in English, however, you usually place a Spanish direct object pronoun before the conjugated verb:

La veo. *(I see it.)*

Table 2-3 lists the direct object pronouns in Spanish.

Table 2-3	Spanish Direct Object Pronouns		
Singular Pronouns	*Meaning*	*Plural Pronouns*	*Meaning*
me	*me*	**nos**	*us*
te	*you* (familiar)	**os**	*you* (polite)
lo	*him, it, you*	**los**	*them, you*
la	*her, it, you*	**las**	*them, you*

Here are some example sentences that show how you use Spanish direct object pronouns:

Él me comprende. *(He understands me.)*

¿Nos ve Ud.? *(Do you see us?)*

¿Los periódicos? Yo los leo cada día. *(The newspapers? I read them every day.)*

People often use **le** rather than **lo** in Spain to express *you* (masculine) or *him.* **Lo** is used as a direct object pronoun in Spanish America. The plural of **lo** and **le** is **los,** which means *them* or *you.* Here are some examples:

- **Cuido al niño.** *(I watch the child.)*
  Lo [Le] cuido. *(I watch him.)*
- **Cuido a los niños.** *(I watch the children.)*
  Los [Les] cuido. *(I watch them.)*
- **Miro el programa.** *(I watch the program.)*
  Lo miro. *(I watch it.)*
- **Miro los programas.** *(I watch the programs.)*
  Los miro. *(I watch them.)*

Understanding the personal a

In Spanish, the personal **a** conveys absolutely no meaning and is used only before a direct object noun (not before a direct object pronoun or any indirect objects) to indicate that it refers to a person or a beloved pet. The following list explains in more detail how to use the personal **a:**

- You use the personal **a** before a common or proper noun that refers to a person or persons. The personal **a** combines with the definite article **el** to form the contraction **al,** but it doesn't combine with the other definite articles:
  No conozco a ellas. *(I don't know them.)*
  Busco al señor Gómez. *(I'm looking for Mr. Gómez.)*

✔ You use the personal **a** before the name of your pooch, tabby, hamster, turtle, or other pet:

Adiestró a Fido. *(She tamed Fido.)*

✔ You use the personal **a** before a pronoun that refers to a person:

No espero a nadie. *(I'm not waiting for anyone.)*

You don't, however, use the personal **a** with the verb **tener** *(to have)*:

Tengo dos hermanos. *(I have two brothers.)*

Coping with indirect object pronouns

Indirect object nouns or *pronouns* refer only to people (and to beloved pets); they answer the question "To or for whom is the subject doing something?" An indirect object pronoun can replace an indirect object noun but also is used in Spanish when the indirect object noun is mentioned. The indirect object pronoun never agrees in gender with the noun to which it refers. And just like with direct object pronouns, indirect object pronouns generally are placed before the conjugated verb. For example:

Le escribo un e-mail. *(I'm writing an e-mail to him.)*

Le escribo a Gloria un e-mail. *(I'm writing an e-mail to Gloria.)*

Table 2-4 presents the indirect object pronouns in Spanish.

Table 2-4	Spanish Indirect Object Pronouns		
Singular Pronouns	*Meaning*	*Plural Pronouns*	*Meaning*
me	to/for me	nos	to/for us
te	to/for you (familiar)	os	to/for you (familiar)
le	to/for him, her, you (formal)	les	to/for them, you (formal)

The following sentences show how you use indirect object pronouns:

> **¿Me dices la verdad?** *(Are you telling me the truth?)*

> **La mujer nos ofrece un refresco.** *(The lady offers us a drink.)*

> **Les doy un abrazo.** *(I give them a hug.)*

A clue that may indicate that you need an indirect object pronoun is the use of the preposition **a (al, a la, a los,** or **a las),** which means *to* or *for* (unlike the personal *a,* which has no meaning — see the preceding section), followed by the name of or reference to a person. You may use **a él, a ella,** or **a Ud.** or the person's name to clarify to whom you're referring:

> ✔ **Yo le escribo a Rosa.** *(I write to Rosa.)*

> **Yo le escribo.** *(I write to her.)*

> ✔ **Ella le habla al muchacho.** *(She speaks to the boy.)*

> **Ella le habla.** *(She speaks to him.)*

> ✔ **Ella le habla a él.** *(She speaks to him.)*

> **Ella le habla a Juan.** *(She speaks to Juan.)*

Although you may use the prepositions *to* and *for* in English, you omit these prepositions in Spanish sentences before an indirect object pronoun:

> **Te compro un regalo.** *(I'm buying a present for you; I'm buying you a present.)*

> **Me escriben.** *(They are writing to me; they are writing me.)*

Choosing the proper pronoun

Sometimes people get confused when trying to figure out whether to use a direct object pronoun or an indirect object pronoun. The good news is you'll have absolutely no problem with **me, te, nos,** and **os** because they act as both direct and indirect object pronouns. They're also reflexive pronouns (see Chapter 3):

> **Me respeta.** *(He respects me.)*

> **Me dice un secreto.** *(He tells me a secret.)*

Nos visita. *(She visits us.)*

Nos trae flores. *(She brings us flowers.)*

Here's one tip: If you can use the word *to* or *for* in an English sentence before a reference to a person — no matter how awkward the construction may seem — you must use an indirect object pronoun in your Spanish sentence:

Quiero mostrarte esta foto. *(I want to show [to] you this photo.)*

The following sections give you some more insider tips that can help you decide between direct and indirect object pronouns.

Common Spanish verbs requiring a direct object

Verbs that require an indirect object in English may require a direct object in Spanish because *to* or *for* is included in the meaning of the infinitive. (Remember that any **a** you see will be the personal **a**; check out "Understanding the personal a" earlier in this chapter.) Some of these high-frequency verbs include the following:

- ✔ **buscar** *(to look for)*
- ✔ **escuchar** *(to listen to)*
- ✔ **esperar** *(to wait for)*
- ✔ **llamar** *(to call)*
- ✔ **mirar** *(to look at)*

The following examples illustrate how you use these verbs:

Nosotros esperamos a nuestros amigos. *(We are waiting for our friends.)*

Nosotros los esperamos. *(We are waiting for them.)*

Common Spanish verbs requiring an indirect object

Verbs that require a direct object in English don't necessarily require a direct object in Spanish. The verbs that follow take indirect objects in Spanish, regardless of the object used in English. This is because *to* or *for* is implied when speaking about a person or because the verb generally is followed by the preposition **a:**

acompañar *(to accompany)*
aconsejar *(to advise)*
contar *(to relate, tell)*
contestar *(to answer)*
dar *(to give)*
decir *(to say, tell)*
enviar *(to send)*
escribir *(to write)*
explicar *(to explain)*
llamar *(to call)*
mandar *(to send)*

obedecer *(to obey)*
ofrecer *(to offer)*
pedir *(to ask)*
preguntar *(to ask)*
presentar *(to introduce)*
prestar *(to lend)*
prohibir *(to forbid)*
prometer *(to promise)*
regalar *(to give a gift)*
telefonear *(to call)*

Here are a few examples:

> **Te aconsejo practicar más.** *(I advise you to practice more.)*
>
> **Ella le pide disculpa a su amiga.** *(She asks her friend for an apology.)*

Doing an about face with gustar

Verbs like **gustar** require special attention because although you can say *I like* in English, in Spanish you have to say that something is pleasing to you. This rule means that Spanish sentences appear somewhat backward to English speakers and that because something is pleasing "to" the subject, **gustar** and verbs like it require the use of an indirect object pronoun. Note how the English and Spanish sentences convey the same meaning but are expressed in a totally different fashion:

English: I like chocolate.

Spanish: Chocolate is pleasing to me.

The following table presents other Spanish verbs that work like **gustar:**

Spanish Verb	Meaning
disgustar	to upset, displease
faltar	to lack, need
fascinar	to fascinate
importar	to be important
interesar	to interest

Spanish Verb	Meaning
parecer	*to seem*
quedar	*to remain to someone, have left*

Here are some examples that show how you use these verbs in Spanish sentences. Note that the subject is now at the end of the sentence and the verb must agree with the subject:

> **¿Te gustan los deportes?** *(Do you like sports?* Literally: *Are sports pleasing to you?)*

> **Nos interesa viajar.** *(We are interested in traveling.* Literally: *Traveling is interesting to us.)*

You use the third-person singular form of any verb from the previous list with one or more infinitives:

> **Me gusta cantar.** *(I like to sing.)*

> **Me gusta cantar y bailar.** *(I like to sing and dance.)*

The following list presents some more details you should know about using these verbs:

- ✔ An indirect object pronoun may be preceded by the preposition **a** + the corresponding prepositional pronoun — **mí, ti, él, ella, Ud, nosotros, vosotros, ellos, ellas, Uds.** — for stress or clarification (see Chapter 4):

  A mí me parece claro. *(It seems clear to me.)*

- ✔ An indirect object pronoun may be preceded by the preposition **a** + the indirect object noun:

  A Miguel no le gusta trabajar. *(Miguel doesn't like to work.)*

- ✔ **A las niñas les gusta el helado.** *(The girls like ice cream.)*

Positioning object pronouns

How do you decide where to place a direct or indirect object pronoun in a Spanish sentence? Generally, you place these pronouns before the conjugated verb:

> **Nosotros los necesitamos.** *(We need them.)*

> **Siempre les cuentas chistes.** *(You always tell them jokes.)*

In sentences with two verbs that follow one subject or in sentences with a present participle (the **-ando** or **-iendo** forms; see Chapter 3), you have the choice of placing the object pronoun before the conjugated verb or after and attached to the infinitive or the participle. The following list provides some examples of this construction.

When you attach the pronoun to the participle, an accent is required on the stressed vowel. In general, to correctly place the accent, you count back three vowels and add the accent. Also, remember that negatives go before the pronoun when it precedes the verb.

* With a present participle:

  (No) Lo estoy haciendo. *(I'm [not] doing it.)*

  (No) Estoy haciéndolo. *(I'm [not] doing it.)*

* With an infinitive:

  (No) Lo quiero hacer. *(I [don't] want to do it.)*

  (No) Quiero hacerlo. *(I [don't] want to do it.)*

In a negative command, the object pronoun precedes the verb. In an affirmative command, however, the object pronoun must follow the verb and be attached to it (for more on commands, refer to Chapter 8). The stressed vowel normally requires an accent mark (if there are only two vowels, no accent is necessary). To properly place the accent, count back three vowels and add it.

Here's what affirmative commands look like:

  Prepárela. *(Prepare it.)*

  Hazlo. *(Do it.)*

Now take a look at the negatives:

  No la prepare. *(Don't prepare it.)*

  No lo hagas. *(Don't do it.)*

Doing double duty

Spanish sentences quite commonly require both a direct and an indirect object pronoun. You have many rules to consider when creating these sentences, as the following list shows:

- ✔ When the verb has two object pronouns, the indirect object pronoun (a person) precedes the direct object pronoun (usually a thing):

    - **Ella nos muestra las revistas.** *(She shows us the magazines.)*

      Ella nos las muestra. *(She shows them to us.)*

    - **Nosotros te damos el boleto.** *(We give you the ticket.)*

      Nosotros te lo damos. *(We give it to you.)*

- ✔ When a sentence has two third-person object pronouns, the indirect object pronouns **le** and **les** change to **se** before the direct object pronouns **lo, la, los,** and **las:**

    - **Él les lee las revistas a sus abuelos.** *(He reads the magazines to his grandparents.)*

      Él se las lee. *(He reads them to them.)*

To clarify the meaning of **se** — because it can mean *to/for you, him, her,* and *them* — you may include the phrase **a Ud. (Uds.), a él (ellos),** or **a ella (ellas):**

Yo se los digo a él (a ella) (a Uds.). *(I tell them to him [her] [you/them].)*

- ✔ The same rules for the positioning of single object pronouns apply for double object pronouns (see the preceding section). The following examples show how you use and place double object pronouns:

    - With an infinitive, you may place the two separate pronouns before the conjugated verb, or you may connect and attach them to the end of the infinitive:

      (No) Te los quiero mostrar. *(I [don't] want to show them to you.)*

      (No) Quiero mostrártelos. *(I [don't] want to show them to you.)*

- With a present participle, you may place the two separate pronouns before the conjugated form of **estar,** or you may connect and attach them to the end of the gerund:

  (No) Se la estoy leyendo a él. *(I'm [not] reading it to him.)*

  (No) Estoy leyéndosela a él. *(I'm [not] reading it to him.)*

- With commands:

  Formal:

  Affirmative: **Dígamelo.** *(Tell it to me.)*

  Negative: **No me lo diga.** *(Don't tell it to me.)*

  Informal:

  Affirmative: **Dímelo.** *(Tell it to me.)*

  Negative: **No me lo digas.** *(Don't tell it to me.)*

✔ When you attach two pronouns to an infinitive, you generally count back three vowels and add an accent:

Yo voy a escribírselo a Ud. *(I'm going to write it to you.)*

When you add two pronouns to a present participle or an affirmative command, however, you generally count back four vowels when adding an accent:

- **Estamos comprándoselas a ellos.** *(We are buying it for them.)*

- **Muéstramelo.** *(Show it to me.)*

With a *diphthong* (two vowels blended together that stand for only one vowel sound), you may have to count back as many as five vowels:

Tráiganoslos. *(Bring them to us.)*

Chapter 3

It's Happening in the Present

In This Chapter

▶ Recognizing different types of verbs

▶ Choosing the appropriate subject pronoun

▶ Conjugating all types of verbs in the present

▶ Communicating in the present progressive

*M*astering the present tense is incredibly helpful because for most people, that's where the action and interest is — in the here and now. In Spanish, you discover that the overwhelming majority of present-tense verbs are very simple to use because they're very predictable. However, you also find out that some verbs walk to the beat of a different drummer; for these verbs, you have to memorize their patterns or irregularities.

In this chapter, you form the present and present progressive tenses with many types of verbs that enable you to talk and write about events and situations that occur now. We also give you information on using Spanish subject pronouns.

Identifying Types of Verbs

If you're going to have any success dealing with Spanish verbs, you need to be able to identify which of the five following groups a verb belongs to:

✔ **Regular verbs:** These verbs are easy to get along with because they follow the regular conjugation rules for **-ar,** **-er,** and **-ir** verbs.

✔ **Stem-changing verbs:** These verbs morph depending on how you use them in a sentence. You encounter three types of stem-changing verbs, classified according to their stem changes: *e* to *i, e* to *ie,* and *o* to *ue.*

✔ **Spelling-change verbs:** Consonant spelling changes occur in some of the conjugated forms of these verbs. The changes enable the verbs to comply with pronunciation rules of the particular letters. The affected consonants are *c, g,* and *z.*

✔ **Irregular verbs:** These verbs follow no rules and must be memorized.

✔ **Reflexive verbs:** Whenever the subject does something to itself, you use a reflexive verb to express the fact that the action is performed or "reflected back" onto the subject of the sentence.

Selecting Subject Pronouns

A *subject pronoun* is a word used in place of a subject noun. This pronoun identifies who or what is performing the action of the verb.

I, we, you, he, she, it, and *they* are the English subject pronouns. They tell the verb who or what is performing the action, and they dictate the form of the verb you must use. In English, he *shops,* but they *shop.*

Spanish uses nine subject pronouns: **yo, tú, usted, él, ella; nosotros** or **nosotras; vosotros** or **vosotras; ustedes;** and **ellos** or **ellas,** as shown in Table 3-1:

Table 3-1	Spanish Subject Pronouns			
Person	*Singular*	*Meaning*	*Plural*	*Meaning*
1st person	**yo**	*I*	**nosotros** (**nosotras**)	*We*
2nd person informal (familiar)	**tú**	*you*	**vosotros** (**vosotras**)	*You*

Person	Singular	Meaning	Plural	Meaning
2nd person formal (polite)	**usted (Ud.)**	*you*	**ustedes (Uds.)**	*You*
3rd person	**él**	*he*	**ellos**	*they*
	ella	*she*	**ellas**	*they*

Using subject pronouns

Unlike the English subject pronoun *I,* which is always capitalized, the Spanish pronoun **yo** is capitalized only at the beginning of a sentence. You always write the abbreviations **Ud.** and **Uds.** with capital letters, even though you write the English equivalent *you* with a lowercase letter, unless it appears at the beginning of a sentence. When **usted** and **ustedes** aren't abbreviated, they're capitalized only at the beginning of a sentence. Here are some examples:

> **Yo me voy.** *(I'm leaving.)*

> **Eduardo y yo salimos.** *(Edward and I are going out.)*

> **¿Busca Ud. (usted) algo?** *(Are you looking for something?)*

> **¿Uds. (Ustedes) necesitan ayuda?** *(Do you need help?)*

In the following sections, I present sets of pronouns that appear to have the same meaning, and I explain when it's appropriate to use which word.

Tú versus Ud.

You use the familiar subject pronoun **tú** to address one friend, relative, child, or pet, because it's the informal, singular form of *you:*

> **Tú eres mi mejor amigo.** *(You're my best friend.)*

You use **Ud.** to show respect to an older person or when speaking to a stranger or someone you don't know well, because **Ud.** is the formal, singular form of *you:*

> **¿Es Ud. español?** *(Are you Spanish?)*

Although **usted** is usually abbreviated **Ud.** when written, you still pronounce it **usted.** Likewise, although **ustedes** is usually abbreviated **Uds.** when written, you still pronounce it **ustedes.**

Vosotros (vosotras) versus Uds.

Vosotros and **vosotras** are informal (familiar) plural subject pronouns expressing *you.* The **vosotros (vosotras)** form is used primarily in Spain to address more than one friend, relative, child, or pet — the informal, plural form of you. You use **vosotros** when speaking to a group of males or to a combined group of males and females. You use **vosotras** only when speaking to a group of females:

> **¿Vosotros me comprendéis?** *(Do you understand me?)*

Uds. is a plural subject pronoun that also expresses *you.* **Uds.** is used throughout the Spanish-speaking world to show respect to more than one older person or when speaking to multiple strangers or people you don't know well. **Uds.** is the formal, plural form of *you* and replaces the informal, plural **vosotros (vosotras)** in Spanish (Latin, Central, and South) America:

> **Uds. son muy simpáticos.** *(You are very nice.)*

Él versus ella

Él *(he)* refers to one male person; **ella** *(she)* refers to one female person:

> **Él toca la guitarra mientras ella baila.** *(He plays the guitar while she dances.)*

Ellos versus ellas

Ellos *(they)* refers to more than one male or to a combined group of males and females, no matter the number of each gender present. **Ellas** refers to a group of females only:

> **Juan y Jorge (Ellos) escuchan.** *(Juan and Jorge [They] listen.)*

> **Luz y Susana (Ellas) escuchan.** *(Luz and Susana [They] listen.)*

Juan y Luz (Ellos) escuchan. *(Juan and Luz [They] listen.)*

El niño y mil niñas (Ellos) escuchan. *(The boy and 1,000 girls [They] listen.)*

Nosotros (nosotras)

When you're talking about someone else and yourself at the same time, you must use the *we* **(nosotros/nosotras)** form of the verb. **Nosotros** refers to more than one male or to a combined group of males and females, no matter the number of each gender present. **Nosotras** refers to a group of females only:

Jorge y yo (Nosotros) jugamos al tenis. *(Jorge and I [We] play tennis.)*

Ana y yo (Nosotras) jugamos al tenis. *(Ana and I [We] play tennis.)*

Omitting subject pronouns

In English, you use subject pronouns all the time to explain who's doing what. In Spanish, however, you use subject pronouns a lot less frequently because the verb ending generally indicates the subject. If you look ahead to the section that follows, you notice that a verb ending in **-o** must have the subject **yo** no matter the infinitive ending **(-ar, -er, -ir)** because no other verb has an **-o** ending. **Hablo español,** for instance, can only mean *I speak Spanish.*

If, on the other hand, you see **Habla español,** it's unclear whether the subject is **él** *(he),* **ella** *(she),* or **Ud.** *(you)* if the sentence is taken out of context. When given the context, you usually omit the subject pronoun **él** or **ella: Le presento a mi amiga Marta. Habla español.** *(Let me introduce you to my friend Marta. She speaks Spanish.)*

To avoid confusion, you regularly use the subject pronoun **Ud.** to differentiate between *he, she,* and *you:*

¿Habla español? *(Do you [he, she] speak Spanish?)*

Mi novio habla español. Habla bien. *(My boyfriend speaks Spanish. He speaks well.)*

¿Habla Ud. español? *(Do you speak Spanish?)*

You regularly use the subject pronoun **Uds.** for sentences in the plural to differentiate between *they* and *you:*

> **Cantan bien.** *(They [You] sing well.)*
>
> **Mis primos están en el coro. Cantan bien.** *(My cousins are in the chorus. They sing well.)*
>
> **Uds. cantan bien también.** *(You sing well, too.)*

Communicating in the Present Tense

You use the present tense to indicate what a subject is doing or does customarily:

> **Nosotros miramos la televisión cada día.** *(We watch television every day.)*

In Spanish, you can also use the present tense to ask for instructions or to discuss an action that will take place in the future:

> **¿Preparo la cena ahora?** *(Shall I prepare dinner now?)*
>
> **Te veo más tarde.** *(I'll see you later.)*

You also use the present tense with the verb **hacer** *(to make, do)* + **que** to show that an action started in the past and is continuing into the present:

> **¿Cuánto tiempo hace que Ud. estudia el español?** *(How long have you been studying Spanish?)*
>
> **Hace dos años (que estudio el español).** *(I've been studying Spanish for two years.)*

Defining regular verbs

Most verbs are fairly well behaved. They follow the rules. They're predictable, especially in the present tense, which makes them fairly easy to master.

You probably haven't heard the word "conjugation" in any of your English classes, even when you had those pesky grammar lessons, because people automatically conjugate verbs in their native language without even thinking about it. So, what exactly do we mean by conjugation? Plain and simple, *conjugation* refers to changing the *infinitive* of a verb (the "to" form — to smile, for example) to a form that agrees with the subject. "I smile, and he smiles, too."

In Spanish, all verbs end in **-ar, -er,** or **-ir.** Most verbs are regular, which means that all verbs with the same infinitive ending follow the same rules of conjugation. If you memorize the endings for one regular **-ar, -er,** or **-ir** infinitive, you can conjugate all the other regular verbs within that "family."

Here's how it works: Take the infinitive and drop its ending **(-ar, -er,** or **-ir),** and then add the endings for the subject pronouns as indicated in Table 3-2.

Table 3-2   Regular Verb Conjugation in the Present

Subject	-ar Verbs	-er Verbs	-ir Verbs
	ganar *(to earn, to win)*	**beber** *(to drink)*	**decidir** *(to decide)*
yo	gan**o**	beb**o**	decid**o**
tú	gan**as**	beb**es**	decid**es**
él, ella, Ud.	gan**a**	beb**e**	decid**e**
nosotros	gan**amos**	beb**emos**	decid**imos**
vosotros	gan**áis**	beb**éis**	decid**ís**
ellos, ellas, Uds.	gan**an**	beb**en**	decid**en**

Here are some examples of regular verbs in the present tense:

> **¿Gana Ud. bastante dinero?** *(Do you earn enough money?)*
>
> **No bebo café.** *(I don't drink coffee.)*
>
> **Ellos deciden quedarse en casa.** *(They decide to stay home.)*

For your reference, the following tables list many regular verbs that follow this easy conjugation in the present. Common regular **-ar** verbs include

-ar Verb	Meaning	-ar Verb	Meaning
ayudar	to help	necesitar	to need
buscar	to look for	olvidar	to forget
comprar	to buy	pagar	to pay
desear	to desire	preguntar	to ask
escuchar	to listen (to)	regresar	to return
estudiar	to study	telefonear	to phone
hablar	to speak, to talk	tomar	to take
llegar	to arrive	viajar	to travel
mirar	to look at	visitar	to visit

Common **-er** verbs include

-er Verb	Meaning
aprender	to learn
beber	to drink
comer	to eat
correr	to run
creer	to believe
deber	to have to, to owe
leer	to read
prometer	to promise

Common **-ir** verbs include

-ir Verb	Meaning
abrir	to open
asistir	to attend
decidir	to decide
descubrir	to discover
escribir	to write
partir	to divide, to share
subir	to go up, to climb
vivir	to live

Changing verb stems

Some Spanish verbs undergo *stem changes* — internal changes to a vowel to preserve the original sound of the verbs after you add a new ending. In the present tense, all stem changes for these verbs occur in the **yo, tú, él (ella, Ud.),** and **ellos (ellas, Uds.)** forms. You conjugate the **nosotros** and **vosotros** forms in the normal fashion (their stems resemble the infinitive).

Sometimes the conjugation format for stem-changing verbs is referred to as the *boot* because if you were to draw a dark line around the forms that have a stem change, they'd resemble a boot. Check out Figure 3-1 to see what we mean.

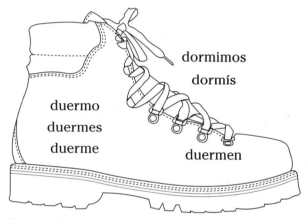

dormimos

dormís

duermo

duermes

duerme

duermen

Figure 3-1: Remember stem-changing verb forms by visualizing a boot.

-ar stem changes

Many Spanish verbs with an **-ar** ending undergo stem changes in all forms except **nosotros** and **vosotros.** The following list details these changes:

- ✔ **e → ie:** For instance, **empezar** *(to begin)* changes to **yo** emp**ie**zo (**nosotros** empezamos). Here are the most frequently used Spanish verbs that fit into this category:

  - cerrar *(to close)*
  - comenzar *(to begin)*
  - despertar *(to wake up)*
  - pensar *(to think)*
  - recomendar *(to recommend)*

✔ **o/u → ue:** For instance, **mostrar** *(to show)* changes to **yo** m**ue**stro (**nosotros** mostramos), and j**u**gar *(to play)* changes to **yo** j**ue**go (**nosotros** jugamos). Here are the most frequently used Spanish verbs that fit into this category:

- ac**o**rdar *(to agree)*
- ac**o**star *(to put to bed)*
- alm**o**rzar *(to eat lunch)*
- c**o**ntar *(to tell)*
- c**o**star *(to cost)*
- enc**o**ntrar *(to meet)*
- pr**o**bar *(to try [on])*
- rec**o**rdar *(to remember)*

Jugar is the only common **-ar** verb whose stem vowel changes from **u** to **ue**.

You use some verbs with stem changes in the present tense impersonally, in the third-person singular only:

Hiela. *(It's freezing.)* **(helar; e → ie)**

Nieva. *(It's snowing.)* **(nevar; e → ie)**

Llueve. *(It's raining.)* **(llover; o → ue)**

Truena. *(It's thundering.)* **(tronar; o → ue)**

-er stem changes

Many Spanish verbs with an **-er** ending undergo stem changes in all forms except **nosotros** and **vosotros.** The following list details these changes:

✔ **e → ie:** For instance, **querer** *(to wish, want)* changes to **yo** qu**ie**ro (**nosotros** queremos). Here are the most frequently used Spanish verbs that fit into this category:

- ent**e**nder *(to understand)*
- p**e**rder *(to lose)*

> ✔ **o → ue:** For instance, **volver** *(to return)* changes to **yo vuelvo** (**nosotros** volvemos). Here are the most frequently used Spanish verbs that fit into this category:
>
> - devolver *(to return)*
> - doler *(to hurt)*
> - poder *(to be able to)*

-ir stem changes

Many Spanish verbs with an **-ir** ending undergo stem changes in all forms except **nosotros** and **vosotros.** The following list outlines these changes:

> ✔ **e → ie:** For instance, **preferir** *(to prefer)* changes to **yo** prefiero (**nosotros** preferimos). Here are the most frequently used Spanish verbs that fit into this category:
>
> - divertir *(to amuse)*
> - mentir *(to lie)*
> - sentir *(to feel, regret)*
> - sugerir *(to suggest)*
>
> ✔ **o → ue:** For instance, **dormir** *(to sleep)* changes to **yo** duermo (**nosotros** dormimos). Another verb conjugated like **dormir** is **morir** *(to die).*
>
> ✔ **e → i (in -ir verbs only):** For instance, **servir** *(to serve)* changes to **yo** sirvo (**nosotros** servimos). Here are the most frequently used Spanish verbs that fit into this category:
>
> - despedir *(to say goodbye to)*
> - pedir *(to ask for)*
> - repetir *(to repeat)*
> - vestir *(to clothe)*

-iar stem change (for some verbs)

Some Spanish verbs with an **-iar** ending undergo a stem change in all forms except **nosotros** and **vosotros.** This stem change is **i → í.** For instance, **guiar** *(to guide)* changes to **yo** guío (**nosotros** guiamos). Here are the most frequently used Spanish verbs that fit into this category:

- ✔ enviar *(to send)*
- ✔ esquiar *(to ski)*
- ✔ fotografiar *(to photograph)*

-uar stem change (for some verbs)

Some Spanish verbs with a **-uar** ending undergo a stem change in all forms except **nosotros** and **vosotros**. This stem change is **u → ú**. For instance, **continuar** *(to continue)* changes to **yo** contin**ú**o (**nosotros** continuamos). **Habituar** *(to accustom someone to)* is another verb that fits into this category.

-uir (not -guir) stem change

Some Spanish verbs with a **-uir** ending (but not a **-guir** ending) undergo a stem change in all forms except **nosotros** and **vosotros**. This stem change is adding a *y* after the *u*. For instance, **concluir** *(to conclude)* changes to **yo** conclu**y**o (**nosotros** concluimos). Here are the most frequently used Spanish verbs that fit into this category:

- ✔ contribuir *(to contribute)*
- ✔ destruir *(to destroy)*
- ✔ incluir *(to include)*

Changing the spelling of verbs

Some Spanish verbs undergo spelling changes to preserve the original sound of the verbs after you add a new ending. This shift is nothing to be overly concerned about because the change occurs only in the first-person singular **(yo)** form of the verb. In the present tense, verbs with the endings listed in Table 3-3 undergo spelling changes.

Table 3-3	Spelling Changes in the Present Tense		
Infinitive Ending	*Spelling Change*	*Verb Examples*	*Present Conjugation*
vowel + **-cer/-cir**	c → zc	ofre**cer** *(to offer)*; tradu**cir** *(to translate)*	yo ofre**zc**o; yo tradu**zc**o
consonant + **-cer/-cir**	c → z	conven**cer** *(to convince)*; espar**cir** *(to spread out)*	yo conven**z**o; yo espar**z**o
-ger/-gir	g → j	esco**ger** *(to choose)*; exi**gir** *(to demand)*	yo esco**j**o; yo exi**j**o
-guir	gu → g	distin**guir** *(to distinguish)*	yo distin**g**o

The majority of the verbs that undergo spelling changes in the present tense end in vowel + **-cer** or vowel + **-cir**. Only a few high-frequency verbs fall under the other categories (**-ger, -gir, -guir**); in all likelihood, you'll see them rarely, if at all.

Here are the verbs with spelling changes in the present tense that you can expect to encounter most often:

Spanish Verb	*Meaning*
aparecer	*to appear*
conocer	*to know (to be acquainted with)*
merecer	*to deserve, merit*
obedecer	*to obey*
parecer	*to seem*
producir	*to produce*
reconocer	*to recognize*

Double or nothing: Verbs with two changes

A few Spanish verbs have both a spelling change and a stem change in the present tense. You must conjugate these verbs to accommodate both changes. Table 3-4 lists these verbs.

Table 3-4	Verbs with Spelling and Stem Changes in the Present Tense	
Verb	**English**	**Conjugation**
corregir	to correct	corrijo, corriges, corrige, corregimos, corregís, corrigen
elegir	to elect	elijo, eliges, elige, elegimos, elegís, eligen
conseguir	to get, obtain	consigo, consigues, consigue, conseguimos, conseguís, consiguen
seguir	to follow	sigo, sigues, sigue, seguimos, seguís, siguen

Using irregular verbs

In Spanish, some present-tense verbs have irregular forms that you must memorize. We cover the three categories of irregular present tense verbs in the following sections: those that are irregular only in the **yo** form, those that are irregular in all forms except **nosotros** and **vosotros,** and those that are completely irregular.

Irregular yo forms

In the present tense, some verbs are irregular only in the first-person singular **(yo)** form. You conjugate the other verb forms in the regular fashion: by dropping the infinitive ending **(-ar, -er,** or **-ir)** and adding the ending that corresponds to the subject. The following table presents the irregular **yo** form of these verbs:

Spanish Verb	Meaning	yo Form of Present Tense
caber	to fit	quepo
caer	to fall	caigo
dar	to give	doy
hacer	to make, to do	hago
poner	to put	pongo
saber	to know a fact, to know how to	sé

Spanish Verb	Meaning	yo Form of Present Tense
salir	*to go out*	**salgo**
traer	*to bring*	**traigo**
valer	*to be worth*	**valgo**
ver	*to see*	**veo**

The following examples show these irregular forms in action:

> **Yo le doy un reloj y él le da aretes.** (*I give her a watch and he gives her earrings.*)

> **Yo me pongo un abrigo y él se pone un suéter.** (*I put on a coat and he puts on a sweater.*)

Irregular yo, tú, él (ella, Ud.), and ellos (ellas, Uds.) forms

In the present tense, the verbs listed in Table 3-5 are irregular in all forms except **nosotros** and **vosotros**.

Table 3-5   Irregular Verbs in All Forms except Nosotros and Vosotros

Verb	Meaning	yo	tú	él	nosotros	vosotros	ellos
decir	*to say, to tell*	**digo**	**dices**	**dice**	**decimos**	**decís**	**dicen**
estar	*to be*	**estoy**	**estás**	**está**	**estamos**	**estáis**	**están**
oler	*to smell*	**huelo**	**hueles**	**huele**	**olemos**	**oléis**	**huelen**
tener	*to have*	**tengo**	**tienes**	**tiene**	**tenemos**	**tenéis**	**tienen**
venir	*to come*	**vengo**	**vienes**	**viene**	**venimos**	**venís**	**vienen**

Tener followed by **que** means *to have to* and shows obligation:

> **Yo tengo que trabajar ahora.** (*I have to work now.*)

Completely (well, almost) irregular verbs

The verbs in Table 3-6 are irregular in all or most of their forms in the present tense.

Table 3-6 Verbs Irregular in All or Most of Their Forms

Verb	Meaning	yo	tú	él	nosotros	vosotros	ellos
ir	to go	voy	vas	va	vamos	vais	van
oír	to hear	oigo	oyes	oye	oímos	oís	oyen
reír	to laugh	río	ríes	ríe	reímos	reís	rien
ser	to be	soy	eres	es	somos	sois	son

Expressing yourself with irregular verbs

The irregular verbs **dar** *(to give)*, **hacer** *(to make, to do)*, and **tener** *(to have)*, as well as a few other irregular verbs, are commonly used in everyday Spanish as part of idiomatic expressions.

High-frequency expressions that use **dar** include the following:

Expression	Meaning
dar un abrazo (a)	*to hug, to embrace*
dar las gracias (a)	*to thank*
dar un paseo	*to take a walk*

Here is an example:

> **Ellos dan un paseo por el parque.** *(They take a walk in the park.)*

High-frequency expressions that use **hacer** include the following:

Expression	Meaning
hacer buen (mal) tiempo	*to be nice (bad) weather*
hacer frío (calor)	*to be cold (hot) weather*
hacer una pregunta	*to ask a question*
hacer una visita	*to pay a visit*
hacer un viaje	*to take a trip*
hacer viento	*to be windy*

Here are some examples of **hacer** expressions:

> **Hace mal tiempo hoy.** *(The weather is bad today.)*
>
> **Hacemos un viaje a Puerto Rico.** *(We are taking a trip to Puerto Rico.)*

High-frequency expressions that use **tener** include the following:

Expression	*Meaning*
tener calor (frío)	*to be warm (cold)*
tener cuidado	*to be careful*
tener dolor de . . .	*to have a . . . ache*
tener éxito	*to succeed*
tener ganas de	*to feel like*
tener hambre (sed)	*to be hungry (thirsty)*
tener lugar	*to take place*
tener miedo de	*to be afraid of*
tener prisa	*to be in a hurry*
tener razón	*to be right*
tener sueño	*to be sleepy*
tener suerte	*to be lucky*

Here are some examples of **tener** expressions:

> **Tengo un dolor de cabeza.** *(I have a headache.)*
>
> **Ellos tienen razón.** *(They are right.)*

 Common expressions that use other verbs that have a spelling change or stem change in the present tense or in another tense include the following:

Expression	*Meaning*
dejar caer	*to drop*
llegar a ser	*to become*
oír decir que	*to hear that*
pensar + infinitive	*to intend*
querer decir	*to mean*

Here is an example:

> **¡Cuidado! Vas a dejar caer el vaso.** *(Be careful! You are going to drop the glass.)*

Recognizing reflexive verbs

Whenever you look at yourself in the mirror or buy yourself something at the mall, you're involved in a reflexive action. You, the subject, are doing something to or for yourself. In English, reflexive actions become a little fuzzy, because so much is considered to be understood. Spanish, however, delineates reflexive action by requiring the use of a reflexive verb.

When creating a reflexive verb construction, you need a subject, a reflexive pronoun, and a verb. When you conjugate reflexive verbs in English, you place the pronouns in front of the conjugated verb. In other words, you say, "You bathe yourself." But in Spanish, the order is *you yourself bathe.*

Are you wondering how to recognize a reflexive verb? It's really quite easy. If an **-ar, -er,** or **-ir** infinitive (which is conjugated in its usual manner) has **-se** attached to its end, you know you have a reflexive verb (**lavarse** *[to wash oneself],* **bañarse** *[to bathe oneself]*). That **-se** ending shows that the reflexive verb has a reflexive pronoun as its direct or indirect object (see Chapter 2). The subject of a reflexive verb, like subjects with other verbs, may be omitted. Whether you use or imply the subject, however, the subject and its reflexive pronoun must refer to the same person or thing:

> **(Yo) Me llamo Gloria.** (*My name is Gloria.* [Literally: *I call myself Gloria.*])

> **(Nosotros) Nos levantamos.** *(We get up.)*

Reflexive pronouns are exactly the same as direct and indirect object pronouns except for the third-person singular and plural **(se)** forms. Because you use **se** when double object pronouns appear in a sentence (as we cover in Chapter 2), remembering to use it as the reflexive pronoun should be relatively easy. Table 3-7 shows reflexive verbs and the reflexive pronoun for each subject.

Table 3-7   Properly Using Reflexive Pronouns

Infinitive	Subject	Reflexive Pronoun	Verb
dormirse (to fall asleep)	yo	me	duermo
despertarse (to wake up)	tú	te	despiertas
desvestirse (to undress)	él, ella, Ud.	se	desviste
lavarse (to wash)	nosostros	nos	lavamos
levantarse (to get up)	vosotros	os	levantáis
bañarse (to go away)	ellos, ellas, Uds.	se	bañan

Some verbs may throw you off a bit. Depending on what you want to say, a verb may have both a reflexive and a non-reflexive form. How's that possible? Well, a reflexive verb requires that the subject act upon itself. What if, however, that subject acts upon someone or something else? In that case, the sentence doesn't need a reflexive pronoun.

Look carefully at the examples that follow:

> **Ella se lava.** *(She washes herself.)*
>
> **Ella lava a su perro.** *(She washes her dog.)*

Conversely, some verbs that generally aren't used reflexively can be made reflexive (if the subject is acting upon itself) by adding a reflexive pronoun:

> **Él prepara la comida.** *(He prepares the meal.)*
>
> **Él se prepara.** *(He prepares himself.)*

The following table presents many common reflexive verbs (letters in parentheses indicate a spelling change).

Verb	Meaning	Verb	Meaning
aburrirse	to become bored	irse	to go away
acostarse (o to ue)	to go to bed	lavarse	to wash oneself
afeitarse	to shave	levantarse	to get up

Verb	Meaning	Verb	Meaning
alegrarse (de)	to be glad	llamarse	to be called, named
bañarse	to bathe oneself	maquillarse	to put on makeup
callarse	to be silent	olvidarse (de)	to forget
cansarse	to become tired	peinarse	to comb one's hair
casarse	to get married	ponerse	to put on, become, place oneself
cepillarse	to brush (hair, teeth)	preocuparse (de)	to worry
despedirse (e to i)	to say goodbye	quedarse	to remain
despertarse (e to ie)	to wake up	quejarse (de)	to complain
desvestirse (e to i)	to get undressed	quitarse	to remove
divertirse (e to ie)	to have fun	reírse (de)	to laugh at
dormirse (o to ue)	to fall asleep	romperse	to break (a part of the body)
ducharse	to take a shower	secarse	to dry oneself
encontrarse (o to ue)	to be located, meet	sentarse (e to ie)	to sit down
enfadarse (con)	to get angry	sentirse (e to ie)	to feel
enojarse	to become angry	vestirse (e to i)	to get dressed
hacerse	to become	volverse (o to ue)	to become

To negate a reflexive verb, you put **no** or the proper negative word (see Chapter 2) before the reflexive pronoun:

> ¿**Se enoja Ud. a menudo?** *(Do you often get angry?)*
>
> **No, no me enojo a menudo.** *(No, I don't get angry often.)*
>
> **No me enojo nunca.** *(I never get angry.)*

Just like with direct and indirect object pronouns (refer to Chapter 2), you generally place reflexive pronouns before the conjugated verbs:

> **Ella no se siente bien.** (*She doesn't feel well.*)

In sentences with two verbs that follow one subject (as in the first two examples that follow) or in sentences with a present participle (see the second two examples here and the following section), you have the choice of placing the reflexive pronoun before the conjugated verb or after and attached to the infinitive or the present participle. When you attach the pronoun to a present participle, an accent is required on the stressed vowel.

> **(No) Voy a maquillar<u>me</u>.** (*I'm [not] going to put on my make-up.*)

> **(No) <u>Me</u> voy a maquillar.** (*I'm [not] going to put on my make-up.*)

> **(No) Estoy maquillándo<u>me</u>.** (*I am [not] putting on my make-up.*)

> **(No) <u>Me</u> estoy maquillando.** (*I am [not] putting on my make-up*)

Making Progress with the Present Progressive

You can use the simple present tense to describe a current action or an action that you perform on a regular basis. But you can also express the same present action as something that's taking place right now by using the *present progressive*. To form the present progressive, you need a form of **estar** *(to be)* and a present participle. We explain both parts of this equation in the following sections.

Understanding present participles

Present participles are verb forms that end in *-ing*. A Spanish present participle has two English equivalents:

✔ It may represent the English for "while" or "by" + a *present participle* (an English verb form ending in *-ing*):

Estudiando, él salió bien en su examen. *(By studying, he passed his test.)*

✔ It may represent an English *present participle* used as an adjective that ends in *-ing:*

Esa niña, quien está tocando el piano, es mi hermana. *(That girl playing the piano is my sister.)*

A Spanish present participle, unlike an English *gerund* (*-ing* verb acting as a noun), may not be used as a noun subject. Spanish uses the infinitive form instead. In the example that follows, the English verb "swimming" is the noun subject of the verb "is." Note the Spanish use of the infinitive, **nadar:**

Nadar es mi pasatiempo favorito. *(Swimming is my favorite pastime.)*

Forming the present participles of regular verbs

Forming participles of regular verbs is quite easy, because participles have only one form. Here's all you have to do:

✔ Drop the **-ar** from **-ar** verb infinitives and add **-ando** (the equivalent of the English *-ing*).

✔ Drop the **-er** or **-ir** from **-er** or **-ir** verb infinitives, respectively, and add **-iendo** (the equivalent of the English *-ing*).

The following table shows these changes for some example verbs:

Ending	Verb	Meaning	Pres. Participle	Meaning
-ar	habl~~ar~~	*to speak*	habl**ando**	*speaking*
-er	aprend~~er~~	*to learn*	aprend**iendo**	*learning*
-ir	escrib~~ir~~	*to write*	escrib**iendo**	*writing*

Be careful! If an **-er** or **-ir** verb stem ends in a vowel, you must drop the ending and add **-yendo** (the Spanish equivalent of *-ing*) to form the present participle:

caer *(to fall):* ca**yendo**

construir *(to build):* constru**yendo**

creer *(to believe):* cre**yendo**

leer *(to read):* le**yendo**

oír *(to hear):* o**yendo**

traer *(to bring):* tra**yendo**

Forming the present participles of stem-changing and irregular verbs

You form the present participle of a stem-changing **-ir** verb by changing the vowel in the stem from **-e** to **-i** or from **-o** to **-u,** dropping the **-ir** infinitive ending, and adding the proper ending for a present participle. (Flip to "Changing verb stems" and "Using irregular verbs" earlier in this chapter for more on these verb types, and check out the preceding section for instructions on forming present participles.)

From **e → i:**

decir *(to say, to tell)* → d**i**ciendo *(saying, telling)*

mentir *(to lie)* → m**i**ntiendo *(lying)*

pedir *(to ask)* → p**i**diendo *(asking)*

repetir *(to repeat)* → rep**i**tiendo *(repeating)*

sentir *(to feel)* → s**i**ntiendo *(feeling)*

servir *(to serve)* → s**i**rviendo *(serving)*

venir *(to come)* → v**i**niendo *(coming)*

From **o → u:**

dormir *(to sleep)* → d**u**rmiendo *(sleeping)*

morir *(to die)* → m**u**riendo *(dying)*

Only three Spanish verbs have irregular present participles. You don't use them very frequently, but you should still be aware of their forms. Yes, you have to memorize them in case you need to use them; at least you only have to worry about three! Here they are:

- **ir** *(to go):* **yendo**
- **poder** *(to be able):* **pudiendo**
- **reír** *(to laugh):* **riendo**

Using estar to form the present progressive

Estar *(to be)* is the verb you most often use to form the present progressive because the present tense of **estar** expresses that something is taking place. The following table presents the present tense conjugation of this irregular verb, which you must commit to memory:

estar *(to be)*	
yo **estoy**	nosotros **estamos**
tú **estás**	vosotros **estáis**
él, ella, Ud. **está**	ellos, ellas, Uds. **están**

You form the present progressive by taking the present tense of the verb **estar** and the present participle of the action verb (see the preceding section). When you put these two together, you have *to be* + doing the action. Here are some examples:

El niño está durmiendo. *(The child is sleeping.)*

Estamos escuchando. *(We are listening.)*

Chapter 4

Spicing Up Your Descriptions with Adjectives, Adverbs, and Prepositions

● ●

In This Chapter

▶ Understanding adjectives

▶ Using adverbs

▶ Comparing things

▶ Joining with prepositions

● ●

*T*his chapter illustrates how adjectives in Spanish are different from adjectives in English and presents all that you need to know to use them properly. You also discover how to form and place adverbs within Spanish sentences. We also include an explanation on how to compare and contrast people, places, things, ideas, and activities. Finally, we introduce you to common Spanish prepositions and explain how to select the most appropriate preposition for your sentences, and how to use special pronouns that follow prepositions.

Adding Color with Adjectives

The function of an adjective is to describe a noun or pronoun so that your audience gains a better understanding of what that noun or pronoun is like. Is the house *big?* Are the trees *green?* You should use adjectives frequently so that people will have the most information about, and the best possible understanding of, what you want to describe. The following sections show you how to use adjectives by discussing their agreement and positioning in sentences.

Making adjectives agree

Unlike in English, where adjectives have only one form, Spanish adjectives agree in gender (masculine or feminine) and number (singular or plural) with the nouns they describe. When the noun or pronoun is changed from masculine to feminine, the adjective describing it must also be changed from masculine to feminine. When the noun or pronoun is changed from singular to plural, its verb and any adjectives describing it must also be changed from singular to plural.

The gender of adjectives

Spanish adjectives that end in **-o,** like most nouns, are masculine. (In some instances, however, masculine adjectives end in another vowel and maybe even in a consonant; see the following section.) As you may expect, a masculine, singular adjective ending in **-o** forms its feminine counterpart by changing **-o** to **-a.**

The following table lists many common adjectives that you may find especially useful in Spanish.

Masculine	Feminine	Meaning
aburrido	aburrida	*boring*
alto	alta	*tall*
bajo	baja	*short*
bonito	bonita	*pretty*
bueno	buena	*good*
delgado	delgada	*thin*
delicioso	deliciosa	*delicious*
divertido	divertida	*fun*
enfermo	enferma	*sick*
enojado	enojada	*angry*
famoso	famosa	*famous*

Masculine	*Feminine*	*Meaning*
feo	fea	*ugly*
flaco	flaca	*thin*
generoso	generosa	*generous*
gordo	gorda	*fat*
guapo	guapa	*pretty, good-looking*
listo	lista	*ready*
magnífico	magnífica	*magnificent*
malo	mala	*bad*
moderno	moderna	*modern*
moreno	morena	*dark-haired*
necesario	necesaria	*necessary*
nuevo	nueva	*new*
ordinario	ordinaria	*ordinary*
peligroso	peligrosa	*dangerous*
pequeño	pequeña	*small*
perezoso	perezosa	*lazy*
perfecto	perfecta	*perfect*
rico	rica	*rich*
rubio	rubia	*blond*
serio	seria	*serious*
simpatico	simpática	*nice*
sincero	sincera	*sincere*
tímido	tímida	*shy*
todo	toda	*all*
viejo	vieja	*old*

Here's an example of an adjective in action:

> **Mi primo Jaime es tímido, y mi prima Francisca es tímida también.** *(My cousin Jaime is shy, and my cousin Francisca is shy, too.)*

Exceptions to the rules

Every rule has some exceptions. In Spanish, masculine, singular adjectives may end in **-a, -e,** or a consonant (other than **-or**). The adjectives in Table 4-1 don't change in their feminine form.

Table 4-1	Adjectives that End in -a or -e	
Masculine	*Feminine*	*Meaning*
egoísta	egoísta	*selfish*
optimista	optimista	*optimistic*
pesimista	pesimista	*pessimistic*
alegre	alegre	*happy*
amable	amable	*nice*
elegante	elegante	*elegant*
excelente	excelente	*excellent*
grande	grande	*big*
importante	importante	*important*
inteligente	inteligente	*intelligent*
interesante	interesante	*interesting*
pobre	pobre	*poor*
triste	triste	*sad*

Here's an example of one of these adjectives at work:

> **Ana es amable, y Pablo es amable también.** *(Ana is nice, and Pablo is nice, too.)*

And the adjectives in Table 4-2 end in consonants and undergo no change for gender.

Table 4-2	Adjectives that End in Consonants	
Masculine	*Feminine*	*Meaning*
cortés	cortés	*courteous*
azul	azul	*blue*
débil	débil	*weak*
fácil	fácil	*easy*
genial	genial	*pleasant*
puntual	puntual	*punctual*
tropical	tropical	*tropical*
joven	joven	*young*
popular	popular	*popular*

Here's an example of one of these adjectives at work:

> **Mi padre es joven, y mi madre es joven también.** *(My father is young, and my mother is young, too.)*

In Spanish, some adjectives of nationality with a masculine form that ends in a consonant add **-a** to form the feminine. The adjectives **inglés** (and other adjectives of nationality that end in **-és**) and **alemán** also drop the accent on their final vowel to maintain their original stresses:

Masculine	*Feminine*	*Meaning*
español	española	*Spanish*
inglés	inglesa	*English*
alemán	alemana	*German*

And some adjectives with a masculine form ending in **-or** add **-a** to form the feminine:

Masculine	*Feminine*	*Meaning*
hablador	habladora	*talkative*
trabjador	trabajadora	*hard-working*

Here are some examples:

> **Fritz es alemán, y Heidi es alemana también.** *(Fritz is German, and Heidi is German, too.)*

> **Carlota es trabajadora, pero su hermano no es traba-jador.** *(Carlota is hard-working, but her brother isn't hard-working.)*

The plural of adjectives

You have to follow two basic rules to form the plural of adjectives in Spanish. First, you add **-s** to singular adjectives ending in a vowel:

Singular	*Plural*	*Meaning*
alto	altos	*tall*
rubia	rubias	*blond*
interesante	interesantes	*interesting*

Second, you add **-es** to singular adjectives ending in a consonant:

Singular	Plural	Meaning
fácil	fáciles	easy
trabajador	trabajadores	hard-working

Just like with some nouns and pronouns, make sure to use the masculine form of the adjective when speaking about mixed company (males and females, with no mind to number):

Mi hermana y mis hermanos son rubios. *(My sister and my brothers are blond.)*

Some singular Spanish adjectives don't follow the basic rules for making plurals. They follow the same or similar rules for plural formation as Spanish nouns (which we cover in Chapter 2):

✔ Singular adjectives ending in **-z** change **-z** to **-c** in the plural:

- **feliz** → **felices** *(happy)*

✔ Some adjectives add or drop an accent mark to maintain original stress:

- **joven** → **jóvenes** *(young)*
- **inglés** → **ingleses** *(English)*
- **alemán** → **alemanes** *(German)*

Positioning adjectives

In Spanish, adjectives may precede or follow the noun they modify. Most adjectives follow the noun. The placement depends on the type of adjective being used, the connotation the speaker wants to convey, and the emphasis being used. And sometimes, when more than one adjective describes a noun, the rules for placement vary according to the type of adjectives being used. For example, possessive adjectives, demonstrative adjectives, and adjectives of quantity precede the noun they modify, whereas descriptive adjectives generally follow the noun they modify. The following sections dig deeper into these topics.

Adjectives that follow the noun

In Spanish, most descriptive adjectives follow the noun they modify. The descriptive adjectives **blanca, feos,** and **interesantes** follow the noun:

una casa blanca (*a white house*)

dos gatos feos (*two ugly cats*)

algunas cosas interesantes (*some interesting things*)

Adjectives that precede the noun

Adjectives that impose limits — numbers, possessive adjectives, demonstrative adjectives, and adjectives of quantity — usually precede the noun they modify. The possessive adjective **su** and the number **una** precede the noun, for instance:

su novia francesa (*his French girlfriend*)

una compañía próspera (*a successful company*)

Descriptive adjectives that emphasize qualities or inherent characteristics appear before the noun:

Tenemos buenos recuerdos de su fiesta. (*We have good memories of her party.*)

In this example, the speaker is emphasizing the quality of the memories.

Shortening certain adjectives

Some Spanish adjectives get shortened in certain situations. The following list details when this occurs:

✔ The following adjectives drop their final **-o** before a masculine, singular noun. **Alguno** and **ninguno** add an accent to the **-u** when the **-o** is dropped:

- **uno** (*one*) → **un coche** (*one car*)
- **bueno** (*good*) → **un buen viaje** (*a good trip*)
- **malo** (*bad*) → **un mal muchacho** (*a bad boy*)
- **primero** (*first*) → **el primer acto** (*the first act*)
- **tercero** (*third*) → **el tercer presidente** (*the third president*)
- **alguno** (*some*) → **algún día** (*some day*)
- **ninguno** (*no*) → **ningún hombre** (*no man*)

When a preposition separates the adjective from its noun, you use the original form of the adjective (don't drop the **-o**):

- **uno de tus primos** (*one of your cousins*)

✔ **Grande** becomes **gran** (*great, important, famous*) before a singular masculine or feminine noun:

- **un gran profesor** (*a great teacher* [male])
- **una gran profesora** (*a great teacher* [female])

But it remains **grande** after the noun:

- **un escritorio grande** (*a large desk*)
- **una mesa grande** (*a large table*)

✔ **Ciento** (*one hundred*) becomes **cien** before nouns and before the numbers **mil** and **millones:**

- **cien hombres y cien mujeres** (*one hundred men and one hundred women*)
- **cien mil habitantes** (*one hundred thousand inhabitants*)
- **cien millones de euros** (*one hundred million euros*)

Describing Actions with Adverbs

The function of an adverb is to describe a verb, another adverb, or an adjective. Does a person run (very) quickly? Is her house very big? You use adverbs to express the manner in which things are done.

Forming adverbs

Many English adverbs end in *-ly,* and the equivalent Spanish ending is **-mente.** To form an adverb in Spanish, you add **-mente** to the feminine singular form of an adjective. Table 4-3 illustrates how it's done.

Unlike adjectives, which require agreement in gender and number with the noun they describe, adverbs require no agreement because they modify a verb and not a noun or pronoun.

Table 4-3	Forming Various Types of Adverbs		
Masc. Adj.	*Fem. Adj.*	*Adverb*	*Meaning*
completo	completa	completamente	*completely*
lento	lenta	lentamente	*slowly*
rápido	rápida	rápidamente	*quickly*
frecuente	frecuente	frecuentemente	*frequently*
especial	especial	especialmente	*especially*
final	final	finalmente	*finally*

The following example shows an adverb in action:

Él entra rápidamente, y ella sale rápidamente. *(He enters quickly, and she leaves quickly.)*

Adverbial phrases

Sometimes, forming an adverb in Spanish by using the feminine singular form of the adjective is quite awkward. You can use the preposition **con** *(with)* + the noun to form an adverbial phrase, which functions in the same way as an adverb. Here are some examples of how this works:

con + noun	*Adverb*	*Meaning*
con habilidad	**hábilmente**	*skillfully*
con paciencia	**pacientemente**	*patiently*
con rapidez	**rápidamente**	*quickly*
con respeto	**respetuosamente**	*respectfully*

Here's an example of this construction:

Ella habla con respeto (respetuosamente). *(She speaks with respect [respectfully].)*

Simple adverbs

Some adverbs and adverbial expressions aren't formed from adjectives; they're words or phrases in and of themselves. Table 4-4 lists some of the most frequently used expressions that fit this description.

Table 4-4	Frequently Used Unique Adverbial Phrases		
Adverb	**Meaning**	**Adverb**	**Meaning**
a menudo	often	**menos**	less
a veces	sometimes	**mientras**	meanwhile
ahora	now	**más tarde**	later
al fin	finally	**mejor**	better
allá	there	**muy**	very
aquí	here	**peor**	worse
bastante	quite, rather, enough	**poco**	little
casi	almost	**por supuesto**	of course
cerca	near	**pronto**	soon
de nuevo	again	**pues**	then
de repente	suddenly	**siempre**	always
de vez en cuando	from time to time	**sin embargo**	however, nevertheless
demasiado	too	**también**	also, too
despacio	slowly	**tan**	as, so
después	afterward	**tarde**	late
en seguida	immediately	**temprano**	soon, early
lejos	far	**todavía**	still, yet
más	more	**ya**	already

Here's an example of one of these phrases in use:

Él habla español bastante bien. *(He speaks Spanish rather well.)*

Positioning of adverbs

You generally place adverbs directly after the verb they modify. Sometimes, however, the position of the adverb is variable and goes where you'd logically put an English adverb:

¿Hablas español elocuentemente? *(Do you speak Spanish eloquently?)*

Afortunadamente, yo recibí el paquete. *(Fortunately, I received the package.)*

Making Comparisons

You generally make comparisons by using adjectives or adverbs. You can make comparisons of equality or inequality, and you can use superlatives.

Expressing equality

Comparisons of equality show that two things or people are the same. In Spanish, whether you're using an adjective or an adverb, you make the comparison the same way. You use **tan** *(as)* + adjective or adverb + **como** *(as)*, as shown here:

Dolores es tan conscienzuda como Jorge. *(Dolores is as conscientious as Jorge.)*

Ella estudia tan diligentemente como él. *(She studies as diligently as he does.)*

You can make negative comparisons by putting **no** before the verb:

Tú no escuchas tan atentamente como Juan. *(You don't listen as attentively as Juan.)*

Comparisons of inequality

Comparisons of inequality show that two things or people are not the same. As with comparisons of equality, whether you're using an adjective or an adverb, you make the comparison the same way. You create the comparison of inequality with **más** *(more)* or **menos** *(less):*

más (menos) + adjective or adverb + **que** *(than)*

Here are two examples:

> **Diego es más (menos) hablador que yo.** *(Diego is more [less] talkative than I.)*
>
> **Diego habla más (menos) que yo.** *(Diego talks more [less] than I.)*

Best of all: The superlative

The *superlative* shows that something (or someone) is the best or worst of its, his, or her kind. You form the superlatives of adjectives as follows:

> Subject + verb + **el (la, los, las)** + **más (menos)** *(more [less])* + adjective + **de** *(in)*

Here's an example:

> **Ella es la más alta de su clase.** *(She is the tallest in her class.)*

If the sentence contains a direct object, you form the superlative by inserting the noun after **el (la, los, las):**

> **Ella prepara la paella más deliciosa del mundo.** *(She prepares the best paella in the world.)*

Now for the adverbs. Superlatives of adverbs aren't distinguished from their comparative forms (see the preceding comparison sections):

> **Él acepta críticas más (menos) pacientemente que los otros.** *(He accepts criticism more [less] patiently than others.)*

Irregular comparatives

As adjectives, **bueno** *(good)*, **malo** *(bad)*, **grande** *(big)*, and **pequeño** *(small)* have irregular forms in the comparative and superlative. Note that **grande** and **pequeño** each have two different meanings in their comparative and superlative forms. Table 4-5 displays all the changes that these adjectives undergo.

Table 4-5	Irregular Adjectives in the Comparative and Superlative	
Adjective	**Comparative**	**Superlative**
bueno (buena) *(good)*	**mejor** *(better)*	**el (la) mejor** *(the best)*
buenos (buenas)	**mejores**	**los (las) mejores**
malo (mala) *(bad)*	**peor** *(worse)*	**el (la) peor** *(the worst)*
malos (malas)	**peores**	**los (las) peores**
grande *(great, big)*	**mayor** *(older, greater in age or status)*	**el (la) mayor** *(the oldest, greatest)*
	más (menos) grande *(larger [less large in size])*	**el más (menos) grande** *(the largest [the least large])*
pequeño (pequeña) *(small)*	**menor** *(minor, lesser, younger in age or status)*	**el (la) menor** *(the least, the youngest)*
pequeños (pequeñas)	**más (menos) pequeño (pequeña)** *(smaller [less small in size])*	**el (la) más pequeño (pequeña)** *(the smallest)*
	más (menos) pequeños (pequeñas) *(smaller [less small in size])*	**los (las) más (menos) pequeños (pequeñas)** *(the smallest [least small])*

The adverbs **bien** *(well)* and **mal** *(poorly)* become **mejor** *(better)* and **peor** *(worse)*, respectively, in their comparative forms and follow the verb or verb phrase they modify:

> **Tomás juega al fútbol mejor que Javier.** *(Tómas plays soccer better than Javier.)*

> **Ella cocina peor que yo.** *(She cooks worse than I do.)*

The absolute superlative

The *absolute superlative* expresses the ultimate; you use it when no comparison is made. To form this basic construction, you add **-ísimo** (masc.); **-ísima** (fem.); **-ísimos** (masc. plural); or **-ísimas** (fem. plural) to the adjective according to the gender (masculine or feminine) and number (singular or plural) of the noun being described. The meaning is the same as **muy** *(very)* + adjective:

> **La catedral es muy bella. La catedral es bellísima.** *(The cathedral is very beautiful.)*
>
> **Los edificios son muy altos. Los edifícios son altísimos.** *(The buildings are very tall.)*

Here are some more things you need to know to form the absolute superlative:

- ✔ You drop the final vowel of an adjective before adding **-ísimo (-a, -os, -as):**
  - **La casa es grande. La casa es grandísima.** *(The house is very large.)*
- ✔ You use **muchísimo** to express *very much:*
  - **Te adoro muchísimo.** *(I adore you very much.)*
- ✔ Adjectives ending in **-co (-ca), -go (-ga),** or **-z** change **c** to **qu, g** to **gu,** and **z** to **c**, respectively, before adding **-ísimo:**
  - **La torta es muy rica. La torta es riquísima.** *(The pie is very tasty.)*
  - **El suéter es muy largo. El suéter es larguísimo.** *(The sweater is very long.)*
  - **El juez es muy sagaz. El juez es sagacísimo.** *(The judge is very shrewd.)*

Linking with Prepositions

Think of *prepositions* as words that join different words, clauses, or phrases. Prepositions relate elements in a sentence: noun to noun, verb to verb, or verb to noun/pronoun. Prepositions also may contract with articles: **a** + **el** = **al** and **de** + **el** = **del** (as we discuss in Chapter 2).

We list the most useful Spanish prepositions in Table 4-6.

Table 4-6	Common Spanish Prepositions		
Preposition	*Meaning*	*Preposition*	*Meaning*
a	*to, at*	**detrás de**	*behind*
a eso de (+ time)	*about (time)*	**durante**	*during*
a través (de)	*across, through*	**en**	*in, on, by*
acerca de	*about*	**en vez de**	*instead of*
además de	*besides*	**encima de**	*above, on top of*
alrededor de	*around*	**enfrente de**	*opposite, in front of*
antes (de)	*before*	**entre**	*between*
cerca de	*near*	**fuera de**	*outside of*
con	*with*	**hacia**	*toward*
contra	*against*	**hasta**	*until*
de	*of, from, about*	**lejos de**	*far*
debajo de	*beneath, under*	**por**	*for, by*
delante de	*in front of*	**para**	*for*
dentro de	*inside, within*	**según**	*according to*
desde	*since*	**sin**	*without*
después (de)	*after*	**sobre**	*over, above, on, upon*

As you can see in the table, some Spanish prepositions have multiple meanings. The following section explains when to use which word, and then we explain which prepositions and verbs go together.

Selecting the correct preposition

Sometimes, selecting the correct preposition to use in a sentence can be tricky because some prepositions have more than one meaning. Take **a,** for example, which can mean *to* or *at;* **en,** which can mean *at* or *in;* and **por** and **para,** which can both mean *for.* Fortunately, Spanish has some rules that can help you understand when the more common prepositions are appropriate.

A

You use **a,** which means *to* or *at,* to show

✔ Time: **Te llamo a las tres.** *(I'll call you at 3 o'clock.)*

✔ Movement: **Vamos a la playa.** *(We're going to the beach.)*

✔ Location: **Espere a la entrada.** *(Wait at the entrance.)*

✔ Means/manner: **Hágalo a mano.** *(Do it by hand.)*

✔ Price: **Puede comprarlo a cien pesos.** *(You can buy it for 100 pesos.)*

You use the preposition **a** (which contracts with the definite article **el** to become **al**) before a direct object alluding to a person; this usage is the *personal a* we discuss in Chapter 2:

Buscamos al señor Nuñez. *(We are looking for Mr. Nuñez.)*

De

Another preposition with several meanings is **de** (which contracts with the definite article **el** to become **del**). You use **de,** which means *of, from,* or *about,* to show

✔ Possession: **Es el coche de Julio.** *(It's Julio's car.)*

✔ Origin: **Soy de Panamá.** *(I'm from Panama.)*

✔ Material: **Es un anillo de oro.** *(It's a gold ring.)*

✔ Relationship: **Madrid es la capital de España.** *(Madrid is the capital of Spain.)*

✔ Part of a whole: **Toma un trozo de pan.** *(She's taking a piece of bread.)*

✔ A subject: **No encuentro mi libro de arte.** *(I can't find my art book.)*

✔ A superlative: **Es el más alto de todos.** *(He's the tallest of them all.)*

En

The preposition **en** can mean *in, by,* or *on.* You use **en** to show

✔ Time: **Estamos en el otoño.** *(It's [We're in] the fall.)*

✔ Location: **Está en esta calle.** *(It's on that street.)*

✔ Means/manner: **Está escrita en español.** *(It's written in Spanish.)*

✔ Movement: **Entran en el banco.** *(They enter the bank.)*

✔ Means of transport: **Viajan en avión.** *(They are traveling by plane.)*

Hasta

The preposition **hasta,** which means *until* (but which also can have the meaning *to*), shows the following:

✔ Place/location: **Conduzca hasta el semáforo.** *(Drive to the traffic light.)*

✔ Time: **Hasta luego.** *(See you later. [Until then.])*

Para versus por

Now you come to two prepositions that can cause much confusion among students of Spanish. **Por** and **para** both mean *for* in English.

The preposition **para** shows the following:

✔ Destination/place: **Salimos para Madrid.** *(We are leaving for Madrid.)*

✔ Destination/person: **Esto es para Ud.** *(This is for you.)*

✔ A future time limit: **Es para mañana.** *(It's for tomorrow.)*

✔ Purpose/goal: **Nado para divertirme.** *(I swim to have fun.)*

✔ Use/function: **Es un cepillo para el pelo.** *(It's a hair brush.)*

✔ Comparisons: **Para su edad, lee bien.** *(For her age, she reads well.)*

✔ Opinion: **Para mí está demasiado crudo.** *(For me it's too rare.)*

The preposition **por** shows the following:

✔ Motion/place: **Caminan por las calles.** *(They walk through the streets.)*

✔ Means/manner: **Lo envío por correo.** *(I'm sending it by mail.)*

✔ In exchange for/substitution: **Voy a hacerlo por tí.** *(I'm going to do it for you.)*

> ✔ Duration of an action: **Trabajo por una hora.** *(I'm working for an hour.)*
>
> ✔ Indefinite time period: **Duerme por la tarde.** *(He sleeps in the afternoon.)*
>
> ✔ On behalf of: **La firmo por Ud.** *(I am signing it on your behalf.)*
>
> ✔ Per: **Me pagan por día.** *(They pay me per day.)*

You use **por** to express *for* after the verbs **enviar** *(to send)*, **ir** *(to go)*, **mandar** *(to order, send)*, **preguntar** *(to ask)*, **regresar** *(to return)*, **venir** *(to come)*, and **volver** *(to return)*. Here is an example:

> **Ven (Regresa, Vuelve) por tu libro.** *(Come [Return, Come back] for your book.)*

If you're speaking about a means of transportation for a passenger, use **en** rather than **por** to express *by:*

> **Van a la capital en tren.** *(They are going to the capital by train.)*

Using prepositions with verbs

The only verb form in the Spanish language that may follow a preposition is an infinitive. Some Spanish verbs require the preposition **a, de, en,** or **con** before the infinitive. Other Spanish verbs that are followed immediately by the infinitive don't require a preposition. The following sections break down all the categories for you.

Spanish verbs requiring a

Generally, verbs that express beginning, motion, teaching, or learning take **a.** However, many other verbs use this preposition before an infinitive. Table 4-7 shows which Spanish verbs call for the use of **a** before the infinitive.

Table 4-7	Spanish Verbs Requiring a
Infinitive	*Meaning*
acostumbrarse	*to become accustomed to*
aprender	*to learn to*

Infinitive	Meaning
apresurarse	to hurry to
ayudar	to help to
comenzar (ie)	to begin to
correr	to run to
decidirse	to decide to
dedicarse	to devote oneself to
empezar (ie)	to begin to
enseñar	to teach to
ir	to go
llegar	to succeed in
negarse (ie)	to refuse to
obligar	to force to
ponerse	to begin to
venir (ie)	to come to

Here is an example that shows how you use the preposition **a**:

Los niños se apresuran a llegar a tiempo. *(The children hurry to arrive on time.)*

Spanish verbs requiring de

The list of verbs requiring **de** before an infinitive is much shorter than the list for those verbs requiring **a.** Table 4-8 lists the Spanish verbs that are followed by **de** before an infinitive.

Table 4-8	Spanish Verbs Requiring de
Infinitive	Meaning
acabar	to have just
acordarse (ue)	to remember to
alegarse	to be glad
cesar	to stop
dejar	to stop
olvidarse	to forget
tratar	to try to

Here's an example showing you how to use **de** before an infinitive:

Mi mejor amiga dejó de fumar. *(My best friend stopped smoking.)*

Spanish verbs requiring en

The list of verbs that require **en** before an infinitive is even shorter than the others, thankfully! Table 4-9 lists these Spanish verbs:

Table 4-9	Spanish Verbs Requiring en
Infinitive	*Meaning*
consentir (ie)	*to agree to*
consistir	*to consist of*
convenir (ie)	*to agree to*
insistir	*to insist on*
tardar	*to delay in*

This example illustrates how you use **en** before an infinitive:

¿Por qué insistes en partir ahora? *(Why do you insist on leaving now?)*

Spanish verbs requiring con

Table 4-10 shows the short list of Spanish verbs that use **con** before an infinitive:

Table 4-10	Spanish Verbs Requiring con
Infinitive	*Meaning*
contar (ue)	*to count on*
soñar (ue)	*to dream of*

Here is an example:

> **Yo sueño con salir con él.** *(I am dreaming about going out with him.)*

Spanish verbs requiring no preposition

Table 4-11 presents a list of verbs that don't require a preposition and are followed immediately by the infinitive.

Table 4-11	Verbs Requiring No Preposition
Infinitive	*Meaning*
deber	*to must (have to)*
dejar	*to allow to*
desear	*to want, wish to*
esperar	*to hope to*
hacer	*to make (have something done)*
necesitar	*to need to*
oír	*to hear*
pensar (ie)	*to intend to*
poder (ue)	*to be able to*
preferir (ie)	*to prefer to*
querer (ie)	*to want, to wish to*
saber	*to know how to*

Here's an example sentence:

> **Sé tricotar.** *(I know how to knit.)*

Using the right pronoun after a preposition

You must use certain special Spanish pronouns after prepositions. The *prepositional pronoun* acts as the object of a preposition and always follows the preposition. Table 4-12 presents these prepositional pronouns:

Table 4-12	Prepositional Pronouns
Singular	*Plural*
mí *(me)*	**nosotros (nosotras)** (*us;* polite)
ti (*you;* familiar)	**vosotros (vosotras)** (*you;* familiar)
él *(him, it)*	**ellos** (*them;* masculine)
ella *(her, it)*	**ellas** (*them;* feminine)
Ud. (*you;* polite)	**Uds.** (*you;* polite)

Here are some examples to show you how you use these pronouns:

> **Esta carta es para mí, no es para ella.** *(This letter is for me, not for her.)*

> **Juego al tenis con él, no con ella.** *(I play tennis with him, not with her.)*

The prepositional pronouns **mí** and **ti** combine with the preposition **con** as follows:

- ✔ **conmigo:** *with me*
- ✔ **contigo:** *with you*

Here are examples that show how you use these words:

> **¿Puedes ir al cine conmigo?** *(Can you go to the movies with me?)*

> **No puedo ir contigo.** *(I can't go with you.)*

Chapter 5

Making Inquiries

- -

In This Chapter

▶ Getting and receiving a "yes" or a "no"

▶ Asking for and giving information

- -

Sometimes when you ask a question, all you want in return is a simple "yes" or "no" answer — no explanations are necessary. Other times, however, you're really interested in getting information and want all the facts, so you need to know how to properly ask questions in Spanish in order to receive the correct answers. And, of course, many people have questions for you that you need to provide Spanish answers for.

In this chapter, you find out how to obtain all the information you need — from easy "yes" or "no" questions to more detailed inquiries about "who?", "what?", "when?", "where?", "how?", or "why?". With the help of this chapter, you can become proficient at not only asking questions but also giving appropriate answers to the questions others ask you.

Posing a Yes/No Question

Forming a Spanish question that requires a "yes" or "no" answer is very easy. You use three simple methods:

- ✔ Intonation
- ✔ The tag ¿(No es) verdad? *(Isn't that so?)* or ¿Está bien? *(Is that all right?)*
- ✔ Inversion

The following sections break down these methods.

Unlike in English, when you want to write a question in Spanish, you put an upside-down question mark — ¿ — at the beginning of the sentence and a standard question mark — ? — at the end:

> **¿Tiene Ud. sed?** *(Are you thirsty?)*

Also, the words *do* and *does* and sometimes *am, is,* and *are* don't translate from English into Spanish. In Spanish, these words are part of the meaning of the conjugated verb:

> **¿Vienen hoy?** *(Are they coming today?)*

To form a negative question, you simply put **no** before the conjugated Spanish verb:

> **¿No quieres tomar algo?** *(Don't you want to drink something?)*

Intonation

Intonation is by far the easiest way to ask a question in Spanish. If you're speaking, all you need to do is raise your voice at the end of what was a statement and add an imaginary question mark at the end of your thought. When writing, you just write down your thought and put question marks before and after it. It's that simple. Here's an example:

> **¿Ud. quiere tomar algo?** *(Do you want to drink something?)*

The tags "¿No es verdad?" and "¿Está bien?"

¿No es verdad? and **¿Está bien?** are tags that can have a variety of meanings:

- ✔ Isn't that so?
- ✔ Right?
- ✔ Isn't (doesn't) he/she?

✔ Aren't (don't) they?

✔ Aren't (don't) we?

✔ Aren't (don't) you?

You generally place **¿No es verdad?** or **¿Está bien?** at the end of a statement — especially when "yes" is the expected answer:

> **Ud. quiere tomar algo. ¿No es verdad?** *(You want to drink something, don't you?)*

> **Tenemos jugo. ¿Está bien?** *(We have juice. Is that all right?)*

Inversion

Inversion means that you turn something around; you can invert anything from a picture to words in a sentence. When forming a "yes" or "no" question in Spanish, you may invert the word order of the pronoun or the subject noun and its accompanying verb form. The following list details some different considerations when using inversion:

✔ With inversion, pronouns tied to the conjugated verb should remain after it:

- **¿Tiene Ud. sed ?** *(Are you thirsty?)*

- **¿Va ella a tomar té?** *(Is she going to drink tea?)*

✔ If the subject noun or pronoun is followed by two consecutive verbs, put the subject noun or pronoun after the phrase containing the second verb (remember to keep the meaning of the phrase intact):

- **¿Quieren comer Uds.?** *(Do you want to eat?)*

- **¿Prefiere tomar carne Luz?** *(Does Luz prefer to eat meat?)*

In most instances, you omit the subject pronoun in Spanish when the subject is obvious:

- **¿Quieres comer algo ahora?** *(Do you want to eat something now?)*

✔ To ask a negative inverted question, put **no** before the inverted verb and noun or pronoun. For verbs preceded by a direct or indirect object pronoun (see Chapter 2) or for reflexive verbs (see Chapter 3), the pronoun should remain before the conjugated verb:

- **¿No toma frutas tu amigo?** *(Doesn't your friend eat fruit?)*

- **¿No las toma tu amigo?** *(Doesn't your friend eat them?)*

- **¿No se desayuna temprano Alberto?** *(Doesn't Alberto eat breakfast early?)*

Responding to a Yes/No Question

You undoubtedly know how to answer "yes" in Spanish because the word for "yes" is common in pop culture. Answering "no" requires a bit more work, because a simple "no" doesn't always suffice. Sometimes you need to express *nothing, nobody,* or other negative ideas. The following sections cover these topics in detail.

Being positive

Saying "yes" in Spanish is really quite easy. You use **sí** to answer "yes" to a question:

¿Quieres salir conmigo? *(Do you want to go out with me?)*

Sí, con mucho gusto. *(Yes, I'd be delighted.)*

Being negative

The most common negative response to a question is a plain and simple **no** *(no, not)*. Other common negatives, which you may or may not use in conjunction with **no,** include the following:

Spanish	*Negative English Equivalent*
ni . . . ni	*neither . . . nor*
tampoco	*neither, not either*
jamás, nunca	*never, (not) ever*
nadie	*no one, nobody*
ninguno(a)	*no, none, (not) any*
nada	*nothing*

Here's a list that details some general considerations to ponder when answering negatively in Spanish:

✔ In Spanish, you generally place negative words before the conjugated verb:

Nunca comprendo lo que Miguel dice. *(I never understand what Miguel says.)*

Unlike in English, double negatives are perfectly acceptable and sometimes even necessary in common usage for a Spanish sentence. Some sentences may even contain three negatives! For example, **No le creo ni a él ni a ella./ Ni a él ni a ella les creo.** *(I believe neither him nor her.)* If **no** is one of the negatives, it precedes the conjugated verb. When **no** is omitted, the other negative precedes the conjugated verb. Here are some examples of both:

• **No fumo nunca./Nunca fumo.** *(I never smoke.)*

• **No viene nadie./Nadie viene.** *(No one is coming.)*

• **No le escucha a nadie nunca./Nunca le escucha a nadie.** *(He never listens to anyone.)*

✔ When you have two verbs in the negative answer, place **no** before the conjugated verb and put the other negative word after the second verb:

• **No puedo comer ninguna comida picante.** *(I can't eat any spicy food.)*

✔ You may also place negative words before the infinitive of the verb:

• **Él prefiere no ver a nadie.** *(He doesn't want to see anyone.)*

✔ You may use negatives alone (without **no**):

• **¿Qué buscas?** *(What do you want?)*

Nada. *(Nothing.)*

✔ A negative preceded by a preposition (see Chapter 2) retains that preposition when placed before the verb:

• **No habla de nadie./De nadie habla.** *(He doesn't speak about anyone.)*

Using no

To make a sentence negative, you can put **no** before the conjugated verb. If the conjugated verb is preceded by a pronoun, put **no** before the pronoun. You often repeat **no** for emphasis:

> **¿Debe estudiar los verbos ella?** *(Does she have to study the verbs?)*

> **(No,) Ella no los debe estudiar.** *([No,] She doesn't have to study them.)*

Using ni . . . ni

In a **ni . . . ni** *(neither . . . nor)* construction, the sentence usually begins with the word **no.** Each part of the **ni . . . ni** construction precedes the word or words being stressed. Each **ni,** therefore, may be used before a noun, an adjective, or an infinitive:

> **No nos gusta ni el café ni el té.** *(We don't like coffee or tea.)*

> **Su coche no es ni grande ni pequeño.** *(His car is neither big nor little.)*

> **No puedo ni cocinar ni coser.** *(I can neither cook nor sew.)*

Using nadie, nada, nunca, and jamás

You use the negatives **nadie, nada, nunca,** and **jamás** after comparisons (see Chapter 4). Note that the English translation of a Spanish negative may have an opposite meaning:

> **Mi madre cocina mejor que nadie.** *(My mother cooks better than anyone.)*

> **Ella conduce más que nunca.** *(She drives better than ever.)*

> **Quieren visitar España más que nada.** *(They want to visit Spain more than anything.)*

Using ninguno

Ninguno *(no, none [not] any)*, when used before a masculine singular noun, drops the final **-o** and adds an accent to the **u**

(**ningún**). The feminine singular form is **ninguna.** No plural forms exist. Here's an example of its usage:

> ¿**Tiene algunos problemas?** *(Do you have any problems?)*
>
> **No tengo problema ninguno.** *(I don't have a problem.)*
>
> **No tengo ningún problema.** *(I don't have a problem.)*

When used as an adjective, **ninguno/a** may be replaced by **alguno/a,** which is a more emphatic negative. This construction then follows the noun:

> **No tiene ninguna mascota./No tiene mascota alguna.** *(He doesn't have a pet.)*

Question words requiring their opposite in the negative answers

When used in questions, some words require that you use negative words of opposite meaning in the responses. The following table presents these words:

If the question contains	The negative answer should contain
alguien *(someone, anyone)*	**nadie** *(no one, nobody)*
siempre *(always)*	**jamás/nunca** *(never)*
algo *(something)*	**nada** *(nothing)*
también *(also)*	**tampoco** *(neither, either)*
alguno(a) *(some, any)*	**ninguno(a)** *(none, [not] any)*

Here's an example sentence:

> ¿**Ves algo?** *(Do you see something?)*
>
> **No veo nada.** *(I don't see anything.)*

Obtaining the Facts

When a simple "yes" or "no" won't satisfy your curiosity, you need to know how to ask for more information in Spanish. Interrogative adjectives, interrogative adverbs, and interrogative pronouns are the tools that allow you to get all the facts you want and need. Find out how in the following sections.

Using interrogative adjectives

You use the interrogative adjective **¿cuánto?** *(How much?/ How many?)* before a noun when that noun may be counted or measured. **¿Cuánto?** varies and must agree in number and gender with the noun it describes:

	Masculine	*Feminine*
Singular	¿cuánto?	¿cuánta?
Plural	¿cuántos?	¿cuántas?

Here are some examples of **¿cuánto?** in use:

> **¿Cuánto dinero necesitas?** *(How much money do you need?)*
>
> **¿Cuántos dólares ganan por hora?** *(How many dollars do they earn per hour?)*
>
> **¿Cuánta sal echa Ud.?** *(How much salt are you adding?)*
>
> **¿Cuántas horas trabajan?** *(How many hours do they work?)*

 Cuánto, cuánta, cuántos, and **cuántas** may also be used as interrogative pronouns. Check out "Employing Interrogative Pronouns" later in the chapter for more info.

The interrogative adjective **¿qué?,** on the other hand, is invariable (it doesn't change) and refers to a noun that isn't being counted. This word is equivalent to the English interrogative adjectives *what* or *which:*

> **¿Qué idiomas sabes hablar?** *(What [Which] languages do you know how to speak?)*

 You may use a preposition before an interrogative adjective where logical:

> **¿A qué hora sale el tren?** *(At what time does the train leave?)*
>
> **¿Con cuánta frecuencia vas al cine?** *([With how much frequency] How often do you go to the movies?)*

Getting information with interrogative adverbs

You use interrogative adverbs when you need an adverb to ask a question. You often use the interrogative adverbs that follow when using inversion to form questions (see the earlier section "Inversion"):

English Adverb	Spanish Interrogative Adverb
How?	**¿cómo?**
When?	**¿cuándo?**
Where (to)?	**¿dónde?**
Why? (for what reason)	**¿por qué?**
Why? (for what purpose)	**¿para qué?**

Here are a couple of these adverbs at work:

> **¿Cómo va Ud. a la oficina?** *(How do you get to work?)*

> **¿Dónde vive tu hermana?** *(Where does your sister live?)*

You may use a preposition before an interrogative adverb where logical (note that the preposition **a** is attached to the interrogative adverb in the first example):

> **¿Adónde quieren ir los niños?** *(Where do the children want to go?)*

> **¿Para qué sirve esta herramienta?** *(How is this tool used?)*

The interrogative adverb **¿Para qué?** asks about a purpose and, therefore, requires an answer with **para** *(for, to)*:

> **¿Para qué usa Ud. esa brocha?** *(Why [For what purpose] do you use that brush?)*

> **Uso esa brocha para pintar.** *(I use that brush to paint.)*

¿Por qué? asks about a reason and, therefore, requires an answer with **porque** *(because)*:

> **¿Por qué llora el niño?** *(Why [For what reason] is the child crying?)*

> **Llora porque está triste.** *(He's crying because he is sad.)*

Employing interrogative pronouns

You use an interrogative pronoun when a pronoun is needed to ask a question. The following table presents the Spanish equivalents to English pronouns:

English Pronoun	*Spanish Interrogative Pronoun*
Who?	¿quién(es)?
What? (Which one[s]?)	¿cuál(es)?
What?	¿qué?
How much?	¿cuánto?
How many?	¿cuántos(as)?

The following list breaks down the characteristics of the interrogative pronouns in the previous list:

✔ The interrogative pronouns **¿quién(es)?** and **¿cuál(es)?** are variable pronouns and change to agree in number only with the noun they replace:

- **¿Quién(es) llega(n)?** *(Who is arriving?)*

  Raquel llega. *(Raquel is arriving.)*

  Raquel y Domingo llegan. *(Raquel and Domingo are arriving.)*

- **¿Cuál(es) de esta(s) blusa(s) prefieres?** *(Which of these blouses do you prefer?)*

  Prefiero la roja. *(I prefer the red one.)*

  Prefiero las rojas. *(I prefer the red ones.)*

✔ **¿Cuál?** means *what* or *which (one/s)* and asks about a choice or a selection:

- **¿Cuál es tu número de teléfono?** *(What is your phone number?)*

- **¿Cuál de los dos es el mejor?** *(Which [one] of the two is better?)*

- **¿Cuáles son los días de la semana?** *(What are the days of the week?)*

✔ **¿Cuánto?,** when it means *how many,* agrees in both number and gender with the noun being replaced:

- **¿Cuántos toman el examen?** *(How many are taking the test?)*

✔ **¿Cuánto?,** when it means *how much,* and **¿qué?** remain invariable:

- **¿Cuánto vale ese coche?** *(How much is this car worth?)*

- **¿Qué significa esto?** *(What does this mean?)*

✔ A preposition + **quién** refers to people. A preposition + **que** refers to things:

- **¿De quiénes habla Ud.?** *(About whom are you speaking?)*

- **¿De qué habla Ud.?** *(About what are you speaking?)*

- **¿A quién se refiere él?** *(To whom is he referring?)*

- **¿A qué se refiere él?** *(To what is he referring?)*

✔ **¿Qué?** means *what* when it precedes a verb and asks about a definition, description, or an explanation. When **¿qué?** precedes a noun, it expresses *which:*

- **¿Qué hacen durante el verano?** *(What are they doing during the summer?)*

- **¿Qué película quieres ver?** *(Which film do you want to see?)*

Hay *(there is/are* or *is/are there?)* is a present-tense form of the auxiliary verb **haber** *(to have).* You use this verb impersonally both to ask and to answer the question you ask. You can use **hay** by itself or with a preceding question word:

¿(No) Hay un buen restaurante por aquí? *(Is[n't] there a good restaurant nearby?)*

¿Dónde hay un buen restaurante por aquí? *(Where is there a good restaurant nearby?)*

Providing Information

This section is chock full of tips on how to answer questions that ask you for information in Spanish.

✔ When you see a question with **¿Cómo?** *(how, what),* give the information or the explanation that's requested:

- **¿Cómo te llamas?** *(What's your name?)*

  Susana. *(Susana.)*

- **¿Cómo prepara Ud. este plato?** *(How do you pre-pare that dish?)*

  Con mantequilla y crema. *(With butter and cream.)*

✔ When you see a question with **¿Cuánto(a)(s)?** *(how much, many),* you answer with a number, an amount, or a quan-tity (see Chapter 1):

- **¿Cuánto cuesta este coche?** *(How much does this car cost?)*

  Diez mil dólares. *($10,000.)*

- **¿Cuántos huevos necesitas?** *(How many eggs do you need?)*

  Una docena. *(A dozen.)*

✔ When you see a question with **¿Cuándo?** *(when),* you answer with a specific time or an expression of time:

- **¿Cuándo empieza la película?** *(When does the film begin?)*

  En diez minutos. *(In 10 minutes.)*

  A las tres y media. *(At 3:30.)*

  En seguida. *(Immediately.)*

✔ When you see a question with **¿Dónde?** *(where),* you answer with the name of a place. You use the preposition **en** to express *in:*

- **¿Dónde vive Ud.?** *(Where do you live?)*

  En Nueva York. *(In New York.)*

You must use the preposition **a (al, a los, a las)** + the name of a place in your answer to the question **¿adónde?** (**¿a dónde?**) (which translates literally as *to where*):

- **¿Adónde van?** *(Where are they going?)*

  Van al estadio. *(They are going to the stadium.)*

You must use the preposition **de (del, de la, de los)** + the name of a place in your answer to the question **¿de dónde?** (which translates literally as *from where*):

- **¿De dónde es Ud.?** *(Where are you from?)*

  Soy de San Juan. *(I'm from San Juan.)*

For more on prepositions, head to Chapter 4.

✔ When you see a question with **¿Por qué?** *(why)*, answer with **porque** *(because)* + a reason:

- **¿Por qué no trabaja ella?** *(Why isn't she working?)*

  Porque está enferma. *(Because she's sick.)*

✔ When you see a question with **¿Quién?** *(who, whom)*, answer with the name of a person.

If the question contains a preposition — **a, de, con, para,** and so on — you must use that same preposition in the answer:

- **¿A quién espera Ud.?** *(Whom are you waiting for?)*

  A mi novio. *(For my boyfriend.)*

- **¿Con quiénes vives?** *(With whom do you live?)*

  Con mis abuelos. *(With my grandparents.)*

✔ When you see a question with **¿Qué?** *(what)*, answer according to the situation. As with the preceding bullet, if the question contains a preposition, you must use that same preposition in the answer:

- **¿Qué escribes?** *(What are you writing?)*

  Una carta. *(A letter.)*

- **¿Con qué escribes?** *(With what are you writing?)*

  Con un bolígrafo. *(With a ballpoint pen.)*

Chapter 6

Revealing the Past

*W*hat's past is past. Or is it? The past tense can be a little murky in Spanish. Sometimes, an action in the past is complete: It's done, over, kaput. In other cases, past action is a little vaguer. It doesn't relate to a specific event but to a past action that was continuous, ongoing, or habitual — something you "used to do" or "were doing," for example, at no set period or time. In order to effectively understand and use the different past tenses in Spanish, you need to become much more aware of their differences, and this chapter helps you do just that.

Living in the Past

In Spanish, several different tenses allow you to express past actions. One of them is the *preterit,* which expresses an action, event, or state of mind that occurred and was completed at a specific time in the past. (For example, "She closed her book" or "He caught the ball.") If you remember that the action ended at a definite moment, you'll have no trouble using the preterit.

The *imperfect* allows you to give descriptions and to speak about what you were in the habit of doing in the past: "He was swimming (used to, would swim) every day." To put it in a visual sense, if the preterit tense captures a snapshot of a past action with the click of the button, the imperfect tense captures the motion of a past action with a video camera. If you recall that an action extended over an indefinite period of time, you'll have no trouble using the imperfect.

In the following sections, we explain how to form the preterit for regular, stem-changing, and irregular verbs and then tell you when to use it. (We cover the imperfect tense later in the chapter.)

Forming the preterit of regular verbs

Forming the preterit of regular verbs is rather easy, because although they have three different infinitive endings — **-ar, -er,** and **-ir** — you use only two *different sets* of endings for the preterit.

To form the preterit of regular verbs, you drop the **-ar, -er,** or **-ir** infinitive ending and add the preterit endings. The following table shows the conjugation of an **-ar** verb:

mirar *(to look at)*	
yo mir**é**	nosotros mir**amos**
tú mir**aste**	vosotros mir**asteis**
él, ella, Ud. mir**ó**	ellos, ellas, Uds. mir**aron**
Yo miré la televisión. *(I watched television.)*	

Here's the conjugation of an **-er** verb:

beber *(to drink)*	
yo beb**í**	nosotros beb**imos**
tú beb**iste**	vosotros beb**isteis**
él, ella, Ud. beb**ió**	ellos, ellas, Uds. beb**ieron**
Él no bebió nada. *(He didn't drink anything.)*	

Finally, allow us to give you this **-ir** conjugation:

recibir *(to receive)*	
yo recib**í**	nosotros recib**imos**
tú recib**iste**	vosotros recib**isteis**
él, ella, Ud. recib**ió**	ellos, ellas, Uds. recib**ieron**
¿**Qué recibiste?** *(What did you receive?)*	

The **nosotros** preterit forms of **-ar** verbs and **-ir** verbs are the same as their present-tense forms:

Nosotros hablamos. *(We speak; We spoke.)*

Forming the preterit of spelling change verbs

Only two categories of verbs have spelling changes in the preterit tense:

✔ Those with **-car, -gar,** and **-zar** endings.

✔ Those that have a vowel before their **-er** or **-ir** ending.

The following sections dive into these changes.

Verbs ending in -car, -gar, and -zar

Verbs ending in **-car, -gar,** and **-zar** undergo a change, but only in the **yo** form of the preterit, as follows:

c changes to **qu**	**tocar** *(to touch)*	**yo toqué** *(I touched)*
g changes to **gu**	**jugar** *(to play)*	**yo jugué** *(I played)*
z changes to **c**	**empezar** *(to begin)*	**yo empecé** *(I began)*

Here are some examples sentences with verbs with these endings:

Yo expliqué el problema. *(I explained the problem.)*

Yo llegué antes de ellos. *(I arrived before them.)*

Yo almorcé con mis amigos. *(I ate lunch with my friends.)*

Verbs that change i to y

Verbs that contain a vowel immediately preceding their **-er** or **-ir** ending change **i** to **y** in the **él, ella, Ud., ellos, ellas, Uds.** forms. All other forms have an accented *i*: **í.**

Spanish verbs that require the **i** to **y** change:

Verb	Yo	Tú	Él/ Ella/ Ud.	Nosotros	Vosotros	Ellos/ Ellas/ Uds.
caer (to fall)	caí	caíste	cayó	caímos	caísteis	cayeron
creer (to believe)	creí	creíste	creyó	creímos	creísteis	creyeron
leer (to read)	leí	leíste	leyó	leímos	leísteis	leyeron
oír (to hear)	oí	oíste	oyó	oímos	oísteis	oyeron

Here are examples using these verbs:

El turista se cayó. *(The tourist fell.)*

Ellos no me creyeron. *(They didn't believe me.)*

¿Leyó Ud. esto? *(Did you read this?)*

No oyeron nada. *(They didn't hear anything.)*

The **i** to **y** change doesn't hold true for the verb **traer** *(to bring):*

Él no trajo su pasaporte. *(He didn't bring his passport.)*

Verbs ending in **-uir** (**concluir** *[to conclude]*, **destruir** *[to destroy]*, **sustituir** *[to substitute]*, and so on) follow the **i** to **y** change, but they don't accent the **i** in the **tú, nosotros,** or **vosotros** forms:

concluir *(to conclude):* concluí, concluiste, concluyó, concluimos, concluisteis, concluyeron

Here's **concluir** in a sentence:

Ellos concluyeron sus estudios. *(They concluded their studies.)*

Verbs with stem changes

The only verbs with stem changes in the preterit tense are -**ir** infinitive verbs that have a stem change in the present tense (see Chapter 3). Be careful, though! The change is different in the preterit tense than it is in the present. Here's how you form the preterit: Change **e** to **i** or **o** to **u** only in the **él, ella, Ud., ellos, ellas, Uds.** forms. The following table shows what these verbs look like in the preterit tense:

Verb	Yo	Tú	Él/ Ella/ Ud.	Nosotros	Vosotros	Ellos/ Ellas/ Uds.
preferir *(to prefer)* **(e** to **ie)**	**preferí**	**preferiste**	**prefirió**	**preferimos**	**preferisteis**	**prefirieron**
pedir *(to ask)* **(e** to **i)**	**pedí**	**pediste**	**pidió**	**pedimos**	**pedisteis**	**pidieron**
dormir *(to sleep)* **(o** to **ue)**	**dormí**	**dormiste**	**durmió**	**dormimos**	**dormisteis**	**durmieron**

Here are examples using these verbs:

> **Ella prefirió quedarse en casa ese día.** *(She preferred to stay home that day.)*

> **Nosotros pedimos su ayuda.** *(We asked for his help.)*

> **¿Dormiste bien?** *(Did you sleep well?)*

The verbs **reír** *(to laugh)* and **sonreír** *(to smile)* change **e** to **i** in the **él, ella, Ud, ellos, ellas, Uds.** forms, and you add accents to the **tú, nosotros,** and **vosotros** forms. Here's the conjugation:

> **reir** *(to laugh):* **reí, reíste, rió, reímos, reísteis, rieron**

An example follows:

> **Ellas rieron se de él.** *(They laughed at him.)*

Forming the preterit of irregular verbs

Many verbs that are irregular in the present tense also are irregular in the preterit, which makes them easier to recognize as irregular verbs. Some of these irregular verbs may be grouped according to the changes they undergo. Unfortunately, a small number of verbs are completely irregular and must be memorized.

Most irregular verbs fall into categories, which makes them easier to remember. The irregular verbs in the categories in this section have the following endings in the preterit tense:

- ✔ yo: -e
- ✔ tú: -iste
- ✔ él, ella, Ud.: -o
- ✔ nosotros: -imos
- ✔ vosotros: -isteis
- ✔ ellos, ellas, Uds.: ieron (or **-jeron** if the stem ends in **-j**)

Verbs with i in the preterit stem

Some Spanish verbs with an **e** or an **a** in their stems change the **e** or **a** to **i** in the preterit:

Verb	Yo	Tú	Él/ Ella/ Ud.	Nosotros	Vosotros	Ellos/ Ellas/ Uds.
decir *(to say, tell)*	dije	dijiste	dijo	dijimos	dijisteis	dijeron
venir *(to come)*	vine	viniste	vino	vinimos	vinisteis	vinieron
querer *(to wish, want)*	quise	quisiste	quiso	quisimos	quisisteis	quisieron
hacer *(to make, to do)*	hice	hiciste	hizo	hicimos	hicisteis	hicieron

In the third-person singular preterit of **hacer, -c** changes to **-z** to maintain the original sound of the verb.

Examples using these verbs follow:

> **¿Qué dijo Ud.?** *(What did you say?)*
>
> **¿A qué hora vinieron?** *(At what time did they come?)*
>
> **Yo no quise salir anoche.** *(I didn't want to go out last night.)*
>
> **Los muchachos no hicieron nada.** *(The boys didn't do anything.)*

Verbs with u in the preterit stem

Some irregular Spanish verbs with an **a** or an **o** in their stem change the **a** or the **o** to **u**:

Verb	Yo	Tú	Él/ Ella/ Ud.	Nosotros	Vosotros	Ellos/ Ellas/ Uds.
caber *(to fit)*	cupe	cupiste	cupo	cupimos	cupisteis	cupieron
saber *(to know)*	supe	supiste	supo	supimos	supisteis	supieron
poner *(to put)*	puse	pusiste	puso	pusimos	pusisteis	pusieron
poder *(to be able)*	pude	pudiste	pudo	pudimos	pudisteis	pudieron

Here are some example sentences:

> **Nosotros no cupimos todos en el coche.** *(We didn't all fit in the car.)*
>
> **¿Supo Ud. la respuesta?** *(Did you know the answer?)*
>
> **Lo puse en la mesa.** *(I put it on the table.)*
>
> **No pudieron hacerlo.** *(They couldn't do it.)*

Verbs with uv in the preterit stem

Three Spanish verbs use **uv** before their preterit endings. Be careful, though, because **tener** doesn't follow the same pattern as **andar** and **estar.** The preterit endings are added after the initial **t,** and not after the infinitive stem **ten:**

Verb	Yo	Tú	Él/ Ella/ Ud.	Nosotros	Vosotros	Ellos/ Ellas/ Uds.
andar (to walk)	anduve	anduviste	anduvo	anduvimos	anduvisteis	anduvieron
estar (to be)	estuve	estuviste	estuvo	estuvimos	estuvisteis	estuvieron
tener (to have)	tuve	tuviste	tuvo	tuvimos	tuvisteis	tuvieron

Here's how you use these verbs in the preterit:

> **Nosotros anduvimos al teatro.** *(We walked to the theater.)*
>
> **Ayer yo estuve en casa.** *(Yesterday I was at home.)*
>
> **Ella tuvo un catarro.** *(She had a cold.)*

Verbs with j in the preterit stem

Some irregular Spanish verbs have a **j** in their preterit stems. This category includes all verbs that end in **-ducir** as well as the verb **decir** *(to say;* see the earlier section "Verbs with i in the preterit stem"). Note that there's no *i* in the **él, ella, Ud., ellos, ellas,** and **Uds.** endings:

Verb	Yo	Tú	Él/ Ella/ Ud.	Nosotros	Vosotros	Ellos/ Ellas/ Uds.
traer (to bring)	traje	trajiste	trajo	trajimos	trajisteis	trajeron
conducir (to drive)	conduje	condujiste	condujo	condujimos	condujisteis	condujeron

The following sentences show examples of these verbs:

> **Ellos no trajeron sus libros en clase.** *(They didn't bring their books to class.)*
>
> **¿Quién condujo?** *(Who drove?)*

The preterit of dar and ver

The Spanish verbs **dar** and **ver** have the same irregular preterit endings. You drop their respective **-ar** and **-er** infinitive endings and then add their preterit endings to **d-** and **v-:**

Verb	Yo	Tú	Él/ Ella/ Ud.	Nosotros	Vosotros	Ellos/ Ellas/ Uds.
dar *(to give)*	di	diste	dio	dimos	disteis	dieron
ver *(to see)*	vi	viste	vio	vimos	visteis	vieron

Here are a couple of example sentences:

Dimos un paseo por el parque. *(We took a walk in the park.)*

¿Qué vio Ud.? *(What did you see?)*

The preterit of ser and ir

The two irregular verbs **ser** *(to be)* and **ir** *(to go)* have the exact same preterit forms. How can you tell which verb is being used in a sentence? You have to look at the context of the sentence. The highly irregular conjugations of these two verbs are as follows:

ser *(to be);* **ir** *(to go):* **fui, fuiste, fue, fuimos, fuisteis, fueron**

The following examples show you how you can figure out the meaning of the verb in use:

ir: Yo fui al mercado. *(I went to the market.)*

ser: Yo fui el primero en terminar el trabajo. *(I was the first to finish the work.)*

Using the preterit

You can use the preterit tense in many ways to convey past actions, events, or states of mind. You use the preterit to express the following:

✔ An action or event that began at a specific time in the past:

El avión despegó a las seis. *(The plane took off at 6 o'clock.)*

✔ An action or event that was completed at a specific time in the past:

Anoche fuimos a una fiesta. *(Last night we went to a party.)*

✔ An action or event that was completed in the past within a specific time period:

Preparé la cena. *(I prepared dinner.)*

✔ A series of events that were completed within a definite time period in the past:

Me desperté, me bañé, y me vestí antes de desayunarme. *(I woke up, I bathed, and I got dressed before eating breakfast.)*

Looking Back with the Imperfect

The imperfect tense is vague and imprecise. That's why it's called *imperfect*. When you know something happened in the past, but you're not really sure when or how often, you use the *imperfect tense.* In English, you typically use the expressions *used to* or *always* to describe these actions.

Forming the imperfect of regular verbs

Just like the preterit, forming the imperfect of regular verbs is rather easy. Although there are three different infinitive endings for regular verbs — **-ar, -er,** and **-ir** — you use only two different sets of endings to form the imperfect of these verbs.

You form the imperfect of a regular verb by dropping the **-ar, -er,** or **-ir** infinitive ending and adding the proper imperfect ending, as shown in the tables that follow:

Here's the imperfect conjugation of **-ar** verbs:

mirar *(to look at)*	
yo mir**aba**	nosotros mir**ábamos**
tú mir**abas**	vosotros mir**abais**
él, ella, Ud. mir**aba**	ellos, ellas, Uds. mir**aban**

Here's the imperfect conjugation of **-er** and **-ir** verbs:

beber *(to drink)*	
yo bebía	nosotros bebíamos
tú bebías	vosotros bebíais
él, ella, Ud. bebía	ellos, ellas, Uds. bebían

recibir *(to receive)*	
yo recibía	nosotros recibíamos
tú recibías	vosotros recibíais
él, ella, Ud. recibía	ellos, ellas, Uds. recibían

Here are some examples of the imperfect in action, using regular verbs:

Los turistas admiraban a los animales. *(The tourists were admiring the animals.)*

Los monos comían cacahuetes. *(The monkeys were eating peanuts.)*

Los tigres preferían dormirse. *(The tigers preferred to go to sleep.)*

Forming the imperfect of irregular verbs

Only three Spanish verbs are irregular in the imperfect tense:

Verb	Yo	Tú	Él/ Ella/ Ud.	Nosotros	Vosotros	Ellos/ Ellas/ Uds.
ir *(to go)*	iba	ibas	iba	íbamos	ibais	iban
ser *(to be)*	era	eras	era	éramos	erais	eran
ver *(to see)*	veía	veías	veía	veíamos	veíais	veían

Here are some examples of these verbs in the imperfect:

Nosotros íbamos al restaurante. *(We were going to the restaurant.)*

Él era alto. *(He was tall.)*

Ellas veían a sus amigos los viernes. *(They saw their friends on Fridays.)*

Verbs that usually have stem or spelling changes in other tenses don't change in the imperfect. So you don't have to learn another set of rules or memorize another list of verbs. Hooray!

Using the imperfect

You'll have no problem knowing when to use the imperfect tense if you can remember that the imperfect is a descriptive past tense. You use the imperfect in the following situations:

✔ To describe ongoing or continuous actions in the past (which may or may not have been completed):

- **Yo lo veía todos los días.** *(I saw him every day.)*

✔ To describe repeated or habitual actions that took place in the past:

- **Ella viajaba mucho.** *(She used to travel a lot.)*

✔ To describe an action that continued for an unspecified period of time:

- **Vivíamos en México.** *(We lived in Mexico.)*

✔ To describe a person, place, thing, weather condition, time, day of the week, state of mind, or emotion in the past:

- **Estaba contento.** *(I was happy.)*

- **La casa era muy grande.** *(The house was very big.)*

- **Hacía frío.** *(It was cold.)*

- **Eran las dos.** *(It was two o'clock.)*

- **Era el lunes.** *(It was Monday.)*

- **Quería comprenderlo.** *(I wanted to understand it.)*

- **Creía que no era urgente.** *(He thought it wasn't urgent.)*

✔ To describe actions that took place simultaneously:

- **Yo escuchaba la radio mientras mi amiga miraba la televisión.** *(I was listening to music while my friend was watching television.)*

✔ To describe a situation that was going on in the past when another action or event, expressed by the preterit (covered earlier in this chapter), took place:

- **Yo escuchaba la radio cuando alguien tocó el timbre.** *(I was listening to the radio when someone rang the doorbell.)*

Choosing the Preterit or the Imperfect

The preterit tense expresses an action that was completed at a specific time in the past. You can represent such an event or action by drawing a dot. Boom! The action took place and was completed, and that's the end of it.

The imperfect tense, on the other hand, expresses a past action that continued over an indefinite period of time. You can represent such an action or event with a wavy line: It just kept moving and moving without an end in sight. The action continued over a period of time in the past: It *was* happening, *used to* happen, or *would* (meaning "used to") happen.

In some instances, either the preterit *or* the imperfect is acceptable as a past tense. The tense you use may depend on the meaning you want to convey. For instance, if you want to convey that the action was completed, you can say

Ella estudió. *(She studied.)*

If you want to convey that the action was ongoing or continuous, you can say

Ella estudiaba. *(She was studying.)*

Signaling the preterit

You often use the preterit tense along with words and expressions that specify a time period. Table 6-1 presents many of these common words and expressions.

Table 6-1	Clues to the Preterit Tense
Spanish	*English*
anoche	*last night*
anteayer	*day before yesterday*
ayer	*yesterday*
ayer por la noche	*last night*
de repente	*suddenly*
el año pasado	*last year*
el otro día	*the other day*
el verano pasado	*last summer*
finalmente	*finally*
la semana pasada	*last week*
por fin	*finally*
un día	*one day*
una vez	*one time*

Here are some example sentences that show how you use these words with the preterit:

Anoche me quedé en casa. *(Last night I stayed home.)*

Finalmente, lo terminé. *(Finally, I finished it.)*

Signaling the imperfect

You often use the imperfect tense with words and expressions that imply habitual action or repetition in the past. Table 6-2 lists many of these words and expressions.

Table 6-2	Clues to the Imperfect Tense
Spanish	*English*
a menudo	*often*
a veces	*sometimes*
cada día	*each day, every day*
de vez en cuando	*from time to time*
en general	*generally*
frecuentemente	*frequently*
generalmente	*generally*
habitualmente	*habitually*
normalmente	*normally*
siempre	*always*
todo el tiempo	*all the time*
todos los días	*every day*
usualmente	*usually*

Here are examples that show how you use the imperfect tense with some words and expressions from Table 6-2:

> **Normalmente regresaba a las seis.** *(You normally returned home at 6 o'clock.)*

> **Siempre jugaban al tenis.** *(They always played tennis.)*

Creating the Present Perfect

Each simple tense has a corresponding compound tense. A compound tense makes an action *perfect* or complete. In English, for example, you eat in the present, but you *have eaten* in the present perfect. In other words, you're done eating in the present tense.

Forming the present perfect

Forming the present perfect in Spanish is essentially a two-step process:

1. Begin with the present tense of the helping verb **haber**.

2. Tack on the past participle of the main verb.

Here's **haber** conjugated in the present tense:

yo he	**nosotros hemos**
tú has	**vosotros habéis**
él (ella, Ud.) ha	**ellos (ellas, ustedes) han**

After you have the **haber** form, you need a past participle. Every verb has a *past participle* that expresses a completed action, such as *taken, spoken,* and *danced.* Forming the past participle in English has probably become second nature to you. In Spanish, you simply need to observe the following two rules for forming the regular past participles of **-ar, -er,** and **-ir** verbs:

✔ For **-ar** verbs, drop the **-ar** of the infinitive form and add **-ado.**

✔ For **-er** and **-ir** verbs, drop the **-er** or **-ir** of the infinitive form and add **-ido.**

Forming and using the past participles is equivalent to using *-ed* or *-en* endings in English.

Table 6-3 shows examples of each type of verb.

Table 6-3	Past Participles of Regular Verbs
Infinitive	*Past Participle*
hablar *(to speak)*	**hablado** *(spoken)*
comer *(to eat)*	**comido** *(eaten)*
vivir *(to live)*	**vivido** *(lived)*

If an **-er** or **-ir** stem ends in a vowel, add an accent mark to the *i* as follows;

Verb	Spanish Past Participle	English Past Participle
oír	oído	heard
caer	caído	fallen
creer	creído	believed
leer	leído	read
traer	traído	brought

The following verbs have irregular past participles:

Verb	Spanish Past Participle	English Past Participle
abrir	abierto	opened
cubrir	cubierto	covered
decir	dicho	said
escribir	escrito	written
hacer	hecho	done
morir	muerto	died
poner	puesto	put
romper	roto	broken
ser	sido	been
ver	visto	seen
volver	vuelto	returned

Using the present perfect

After you know how to conjugate the verb **haber** in the present tense and form the past participle of some common verbs, you have everything you need to know to be able to form and use the present perfect.

Keep the following rules and regulations in mind:

- ✔ Use the present perfect to express or describe actions that have happened recently and/or actions that still hold true in the present, as in the sentences: "She has arrived," or "They have lived here for two years (and still do)."

- ✔ Never separate the verb **haber** and the past participle with any other words.

- ✔ When using an object pronoun with the present perfect, the pronoun must precede the conjugated form of the verb **haber**.

The sample sentences in the list that follows show the use of the present perfect:

> **Yo he terminado la carta.** *(I have finished the letter.)*
>
> **Ellos han empezado la casa nueva.** *(They have started the new house.)*
>
> **Ella ha leído aquella novela.** *(She has read that novel.)*

The past participle remains the same for every subject. Only the helping verb changes:

> **Él ha dicho una mentira y ellas han dicho la verdad.** *(He has told a lie and they have told the truth.)*

Chapter 7

Looking to the Future

* *

In This Chapter

▶ Expressing the future in three ways

▶ Forming the future of regular and irregular verbs

▶ Putting the future to use

* *

*T*his chapter allows you to look toward the future. You discover how to use the present tense to express a future action. You practice using the Spanish verb **ir** *(to go)* + the preposition **a** to say what a subject is going to do. And you discover how to form the future of regular and irregular verbs, all with no spelling or stem changes!

Talking about the Future without Using the Future Tense

You can tell someone that something is going to happen in the future without knowing how to create the future tense of a Spanish verb. How cool is that? You can use the present tense in certain situations, and in other situations, you can use **ir** *(to go)* + the preposition **a** + an infinitive. In the following sections, we explain exactly when you can use these non-future constructions to convey the future.

Using the present to express the future

You use the present tense to imply the future when asking for instructions or when the proposed action will take place in the not-so-distant or near future (see Chapter 3). Here are two examples of these usages:

> **¿Dejo de hablar?** *(Shall I stop talking?)*

> **Ellos pasan por nuestra casa.** *(They'll be stopping by our house.)*

Expressing the near future

You use the present tense of the verb **ir** *(to go)* + the preposition **a** (which has no meaning in this particular construction) + the infinitive of the verb to express an action that will be taking place rather soon or that's imminent. First take a quick look at the irregular verb **ir** in the present tense:

ir *(to go)*	
yo **voy**	nosotros **vamos**
tú **vas**	vosotros **vais**
él, ella, Ud. **va**	ellos, ellas, Uds. **van**

Here are some examples that use **ir** + **a** and allow you to express what the subject is going to do in the form of an infinitive:

> **Voy a salir.** *(I'm going to go out.)*

> **Vamos a esperarlos.** *(We are going to wait for them.)*

Mastering the Future Tense

When you want to talk about what a subject will do or what action or event will take place in the not-so-immediate future, you have to use the future tense of the verb. Here's where the conjugation comes in, but don't worry. Forming the future tense is a breeze compared to other verb tenses; you can see what we mean in the following sections on regular and irregular verbs.

Forming the future of regular verbs

The future tense in Spanish is just about as easy to form as possible, because *all* verbs — every single one of them: regular verbs, verbs with spelling and stem changes, and irregular verbs — have the same future endings. Well, some verbs do have irregular future stems, but that's only a few (see the following section for more on these verbs).

To form the future tense of a regular verb, you add the appropriate future ending (dependent on the subject) to the infinitive of the verb:

Future Endings for All Verbs	
yo -**é**	nosotros -**emos**
tú -**ás**	vosotros -**éis**
él, ella, Ud. -**á**	ellos, ellas, Uds. -**án**

The tables that follow show how you use these endings to form the future of regular verbs:

✔ -**ar** verbs:

trabajar *(to work)*	
yo trabajar**é**	nosotros trabajar**emos**
tú trabajar**ás**	vosotros trabajar**éis**
él, ella, Ud. trabajar**á**	ellos, ellas, Uds. trabajar**án**

✔ -**er** verbs:

vender *(to sell)*	
yo vender**é**	nosotros vender**emos**
tú vender**ás**	vosotros vender**éis**
él, ella, Ud. vender**á**	ellos, ellas, Uds. vender**án**

⟋ **-ir** verbs:

discutir *(to discuss, argue)*	
yo discutir**é**	nosotros discutir**emos**
tú discutir**ás**	vosotros discutir**éis**
él, ella, Ud. discutir**á**	ellos, ellas, Uds. discutir**án**

Now check out some example sentences that use the future tense:

> **Yo no los invitaré a mi fiesta.** *(I won't invite them to my party.)*
>
> **Ellos no beberán alcohol.** *(They won't drink alcohol.)*
>
> **¿Abrirás una cuenta bancaria pronto?** *(Will you open a bank account soon?)*

Verbs whose infinitives contain an accent mark over the *i*, such as **oír** *(to listen)* and **reír** *(to laugh),* — drop their accents in the future tense:

> **Yo no oiré esas mentiras.** *(I won't listen to those lies.)*
>
> **Ellos no se reirán de él.** *(They won't laugh at him.)*

When conjugating reflexive verbs in the future tense, the reflexive pronoun goes in front of the conjugated verb form. (Check out Chapter 3 for more on reflexive verbs.)

> **Me acostaré temprano esta noche.** *(I'm going to go to bed early tonight.)*

Forming the future of irregular verbs

Certain Spanish verbs are irregular in the future tense. These verbs have irregular future stems, which always end in **-r** or **-rr** — an easy way to remember them! To form the future of these irregular verbs, you do one of three things:

✔ Drop **e** from the infinitive ending before adding the appropriate future ending:

Infinitive	Meaning	Future Stem
caber	to fit	cabr-
haber	to have	habr-
poder	to be able	podr-
querer	to want	querr-
saber	to know	sabr-

Here are some example sentences:

- **¿Cabrá esa máquina en el gabinete?** *(Will that machine fit in the cabinet?)*

- **No podremos venir.** *(We will not be able to come.)*

✔ Drop **e** or **i** from the infinitive ending and replace the vowel with a **d** before adding the appropriate future ending:

Infinitive	Meaning	Future Stem
poner	to put	pondr-
salir	to leave	saldr-
tener	to have	tendr-
valer	to be worth	valdr-
venir	to come	vendr-

Three of these verbs are illustrated in the following example sentences:

- **¿Cuándo saldrán?** *(When will they leave?)*

- **¿Cuánto valdrá ese coche?** *(How much will that car be worth?)*

- **¿No vendrás mañana?** *(Won't you be coming tomorrow?)*

✔ Memorize the irregular stems and add the appropriate future endings. At this level, you need to know only two high-frequency irregular verbs in Spanish that are irregular in the future:

Infinitive	Meaning	Future Stem
decir	to say	dir-
hacer	to make, to do	har-

Observe these verbs in action:

- **Yo diré lo que pienso.** *(I will say what I think.)*

- **¿Qué harán para resolver el problema?** *(What will they do to solve the problem?)*

Using the Future to Foretell, Predict, and Wonder

Using the future tense to express future time seems kind of obvious. However, you must be aware of other instances in Spanish when you may use the future, too. For instance, you use the future

✔ To predict a future action or event:

- **Lloverá pronto.** *(It will rain soon.)*

✔ To express wonder, probability, conjecture, or uncertainty in the present. The Spanish future, in this case, is the equivalent to the following English phrases: "I wonder," "probably," or "must be."

- **¿Cuánto dinero tendrán?** *(I wonder how much money they have.)*

- **Serán las seis.** *(It's probably [It must be] six o'clock.)*

- **Alguien viene. ¿Quién será?** *(Someone is coming. I wonder who it is?)*

- **¿Será mi esposo?** *(I wonder if it's my husband.)*

- **¿Me dará un anillo mi novio?** *(I wonder if my boyfriend is going to give me a ring.)*

✔ To express something that you expect and that's due to or caused by a present action or event:

- **Si viene a tiempo, el jefe no se quejará.** *(If you come on time, the boss won't complain.)*

- **Si sigues la receta, prepararás una buena comida.** *(If you follow the recipe, you'll prepare a good meal.)*

Chapter 8

Identifying Verb Moods

*I*n other chapters in this book, we cover verb tenses (past, present, future, and so on). In this chapter, we explain different moods of verbs. No, we don't mean angry or excited verbs. A verb's *mood* reflects the subject's attitude toward what the verb expresses. Moods come in four flavors:

✔ The *indicative mood,* the most commonly used, states a fact and requires the present, past, or future tense. (See Chapters 3, 6, and 7 for more on these tenses.)

✔ The *imperative mood* requires a command.

✔ The *subjunctive* is a mood that shows wishing, wanting, emotion, need, or doubt (among other things) and requires special verb forms.

✔ The *conditional mood* indicates what *would* happen under certain circumstances.

In this chapter, we focus on commands, the present and present perfect subjunctive, and the conditional moods.

Giving Commands with the Imperative Mood

When you tell a waiter to bring you water, ask a dinner guest to please pass the salt, or tell your dog to lie down, you're using the imperative mood. You're giving a command — telling someone, or sometimes yourself, to do something.

In most cases, you bark out commands in the *you* form, but remember that in Spanish *you* can mean any of four different *you*s. With the imperative, you can also give what is called a *let's* command, as in, "Let's go to the movie." This less asser-tive form of the imperative takes the **nosotros** form.

Forming commands with Ud. and Uds.

When forming the formal *you* singular, that is, the **usted (Ud.),** commands in the affirmative and the negative forms, you drop the **-o** ending of the **yo** form, and add an **-e** for **-ar** verbs or an **-a** for **-er** and **-ir** verbs. Here are a few examples:

¡Hable! *(Speak!)*	**¡No hable!** *(Don't speak!)*
¡Coma! *(Eat!)*	**¡No coma!** *(Don't eat!)*
¡Escriba! *(Write!)*	**¡No escriba!** *(Don't write!)*

Spanish has only the following three irregular **usted** commands:

Infinitive	Positive Command	Negative Command
ir	**¡Vaya!** *(Go!)*	**¡No vaya!** *(Don't go)*
saber	**¡Sepa!** *(Know!)*	**¡No sepa!** *(Don't know!)*
ser	**¡Sea!** *(Be!)*	**¡No sea!** *(Don't be!)*

The verbs **dar** *(to give)* and **estar** *(to be)* add accents in the following formal command forms to maintain proper stress:

> **dar: ¡Dé (Ud.)!** *(Give!)*
>
> **estar: ¡Esté (Ud.)!** *(Be!)*   **¡Estén (Uds.)!** *(Give!)*

When forming the formal, plural *you* or **ustedes (Uds.)** commands, you simply add an **-n** to the **Ud.** command form. This rule applies for the regular and irregular verbs, as shown in the following examples:

> **Hablen.** *(Speak!)*
>
> **¡No coman!** *(Don't eat!)*
>
> **Escriban.** *(Write!)*
>
> **¡No sean tontos!** *(Don't be foolish!)*

Forming commands with tú and vosotros

You can form positive **tú** commands by dropping the **-s** from the present tense **tú** forms of regular **-ar, -er,** or **-ir** verbs:

- ✔ **Hablas** *(you speak)* becomes **¡Habla!** *(Speak!)*
- ✔ **Comes** *(you eat)* becomes **¡Come!** *(Eat!)*
- ✔ **Escribes** *(you write)* becomes **¡Escribe!** *(Write!)*

You can form negative **tú** commands by taking the **-o** off of the present-tense **yo** form and adding **-es** for regular **-ar** verbs and **-as** for regular **-er** and **-ir** verbs:

- ✔ **Hablo** *(I speak)* becomes **¡No hables!** *(Don't speak!)*
- ✔ **Como** *(I eat)* becomes **¡No comas!** *(Don't eat!)*
- ✔ **Escribo** *(I write)* becomes **¡No escribas!** *(Don't write!)*

Spanish also includes some irregular **tú** form commands. Table 8-1 shows the positive and negative forms of the most common irregular **tú** form commands.

Table 8-1	Irregular Tú Form Commands	
Infinitive	*Positive Command*	*Negative Command*
decir *(to say, tell)*	**Di**	**No digas**
hacer *(to do, make)*	**Haz**	**No hagas**
ir *(to go)*	**Ve**	**No vayas**

(continued)

Table 8-1 *(continued)*

Infinitive	Positive Command	Negative Command
poner *(to put)*	**Pon**	**No pongas**
salir *(to leave)*	**Sal**	**No salgas**
ser *(to be)*	**Sé**	**No seas**
tener *(to have)*	**Ten**	**No tengas**
venir *(to come)*	**Ven**	**No vengas**

Here is an example:

> **¡No tengas miedo sino que ten cuidado!** *(Don't be afraid, but be careful!)*

When forming the positive, informal, plural *you* or **vosotros** commands for regular verbs, you drop the **-r** from the infinitive form and add **-d,** as you can see in the following examples:

> **¡Hablad!** *(Speak!)*
>
> **¡Comed!** *(Eat!)*
>
> **¡Escribid!** *(Write!)*

When forming the negative **vosotros** commands, you simply drop the **-o** from the present-tense **yo** form and add **-éis** for **-ar** verbs or **-áis** for **-er** and **-ir** verbs, as follows:

> **¡No habléis!** *(Don't speak!)*
>
> **¡No comáis!** *(Don't eat!)*
>
> **¡No escribáis!** *(Don't write!)*

The same three verbs are irregular in the negative **vosotros** command forms as in the **usted** forms. They are

Infinitive	*Negative Command*
ir	**¡No vayáis!** *(Don't go!)*
saber	**No sepáis . . .** *(Don't know . . .)*
ser	**No seáis . . .** *(Don't be . . .)*

Dar *(to give)* drops the accent in the negative **vosotros** command: **¡No deis!** *(Don't give!)*

Forming the let's command

The **nosotros-**form commands, or the *let's* commands, enable you to make suggestions to your friends or to a group of people (including yourself) about what you want to do. When forming these commands, take the **-o** off of the present-tense **yo** form of the verb and add **-emos** for **-ar** verbs or **-amos** for **-er** and **-ir** verbs. You simply put **no** in front of the verb to make a negative *let's* command. Some examples follow in Table 8-2.

Table 8-2   *Let's* Commands with Regular Verbs

Infinitive (Ending)	Positive Command	Negative Command
hablar (-ar) *(to speak)*	**Hablemos.**	**No hablemos.**
comer (-er) *(to eat)*	**Comamos.**	**No comamos.**
escribir (-ir) *(to write)*	**Escribamos.**	**No escribamos.**

For example:

> **¡No hablemos! ¡Comamos!** *(Let's not speak! Let's eat!)*

The three verbs in Table 8-3 are irregular in the **nosotros** command form, both in their affirmative and the negative formations. Note that **ir** is different in its affirmative and negative forms.

Table 8-3   *Let's* Commands with Irregular Verbs

Infinitive	Positive Command	Negative Command
ir *(to go)*	**Vamos.**	**No vayamos.**
saber *(to know)*	**Sepamos.**	**No sepamos.**
ser *(to be)*	**Seamos.**	**No seamos.**

An example follows:

> **¡No vayamos al parque! ¡Vamos al cine!** *(Let's not go to the park! Let's go to the movies!)*

Forming the Present Subjunctive

So, you're unfamiliar with the subjunctive. We're not at all surprised — it's not that commonly discussed in English. It indicates how the speaker feels about or perceives a situation rather than when an action occurred. In this section, you discover how to form the present subjunctive (which we sometimes refer to here as just "the subjunctive") of regular verbs, verbs with spelling changes, verbs with stem changes, and completely irregular verbs.

Creating the present subjunctive of regular verbs

You form the present subjunctive of regular verbs by dropping the **-o** from the **yo** form of the present tense and adding the subjunctive endings shown in bold in Table 8-4. These endings are relatively easy to remember, because **-ar** verbs (such as **hablar**) use the present-tense endings of **-er** verbs, and **-er (comprender)** and **-ir (escribir)** verbs use the present-tense endings of **-ar** verbs. This switch is why people say that you form the present subjunctive by using the opposite verb endings on the stem.

Table 8-4	The Present Subjunctive Endings of Regular Verbs		
	-ar verbs	*-er verbs*	*-ir verbs*
yo form of present tense	hable *(I speak)*	comprende *(I understand)*	escribe *(I write)*
yo	habl**e**	comprend**a**	escrib**a**
tú	habl**es**	comprend**as**	escrib**as**
él, ella, Ud.	habl**e**	comprend**a**	escrib**a**
nosotros	habl**emos**	comprend**amos**	escrib**amos**
vosotros	habl**éis**	comprend**áis**	escrib**áis**
ellos, ellas, Uds.	habl**en**	comprend**an**	escrib**an**

Here are some examples of these verbs in the subjunctive:

Es importante que yo hable con sus padres. *(It is important that I speak to your parents.)*

Es esencial que Ud. comprenda las reglas. *(It is essential that you understand the rules.)*

Es necesario que nosotros escribamos las notas. *(It is necessary that we write the notes.)*

Working with verbs irregular in the yo form

Some verbs are irregular in the **yo** form of the present tense. These verbs use the stem of the **yo** to form the present subjunctive. You drop the final **-o** from the **yo** form and add the opposite endings. In other words, you add an ending that starts with **-a** for the **-er** and **-ir** verbs listed in Table 8-5.

Table 8-5	Subjunctive Stems Derived from the Present-Tense yo Form	
Verb	*yo Form*	*Subjunctive Forms*
caber *(to fit)*	**quepo**	quep**a**, quep**as**, quep**a**, quep**amos**, quep**áis**, quep**an**
caer *(to fall)*	**caigo**	caig**a**, caig**as**, caig**a**, caig**amos**, caig**áis**, caig**an**
decir *(to say, to tell)*	**digo**	dig**a**, dig**as**, dig**a**, dig**amos**, dig**áis**, dig**an**
hacer *(to make, to do)*	**hago**	hag**a**, hag**as**, hag**a**, hag**amos**, hag**áis**, hag**an**
oír *(to hear)*	**oigo**	oig**a**, oig**as**, oig**a**, oig**amos**, oig**áis**, oig**an**
poner *(to put)*	**pongo**	pong**a**, pong**as**, pong**a**, pong**amos**, pong**áis**, pong**an**
salir *(to go out)*	**salgo**	salg**a**, salg**as**, salg**a**, salg**amos**, salg**áis**, salg**an**
tener *(to have)*	**tengo**	teng**a**, teng**as**, teng**a**, teng**amos**, teng**áis**, teng**an**

(continued)

Table 8-5 *(continued)*

Verb	yo Form	Subjunctive Forms
traer *(to bring)*	**traigo**	traig**a**, traig**as**, traig**a**, traig**amos**, traig**áis**, traig**an**
valer *(to be worth)*	**valgo**	valg**a**, valg**as**, valg**a**, valg**amos**, valg**áis**, valg**an**
venir *(to come)*	**vengo**	veng**a**, veng**as**, veng**a**, veng**amos**, veng**áis**, veng**an**
ver *(to see)*	**veo**	ve**a**, ve**as**, ve**a**, ve**amos**, ve**áis**, ve**an**

Here are some examples of these types of verbs:

> **Es imposible que todo quepa en mi maleta.** *(It's impossible that everything will fit in my suitcase.)*

> **Es urgente que Uds. hagan todo este trabajo ahora.** *(It is urgent that you do all this work now.)*

Tackling verbs with spelling changes

Some Spanish verbs have the same spelling change in the present subjunctive as they have in the present tense. Namely, verbs ending in **-cer/-cir**, **-ger/-gir**, and **-guir** (not **-uir**) undergo the same changes that occur in the **yo** form of the present. These changes are as follows:

- ✔ vowel + **-cer/-cir** verbs: **c → zc**
- ✔ consonant + **-cer /-cir** verbs: **c → z**
- ✔ **-ger/-gir** verbs: **g → j**
- ✔ **-guir** verbs: **gu → g**

Use the regular subjunctive ending after making the spelling changes shown in Table 8-6.

Table 8-6	Present Subjunctive of Verbs with Spelling Changes	
Infinitive	*Present yo Form*	*Stem*
ofrecer *(to offer)*	**ofrezco**	**ofrezc-**
traducir *(to translate)*	**traduzco**	**traduzc-**
convencer *(to convince)*	**convenzo**	**convenz-**
esparcir *(to spread)*	**esparzo**	**esparz-**
escoger *(to choose)*	**escojo**	**escoj-**
exigir *(to demand)*	**exijo**	**exij-**
distinguir *(to distinguish)*	**distingo**	**disting-**

The following examples illustrate these spelling changes:

> **Es una lástima que el director no le ofrezca un aumento de salario.** *(It is a pity that the director isn't offering him a raise.)*

> **Es natural que el jefe exija mucho de sus empleados.** *(It is natural that the boss demands a lot from his employees.)*

You see some different spelling changes for verbs in the present subjunctive than you see for verbs with spelling changes in the present tense. In the present subjunctive, verbs ending in **-car, -gar,** and **-zar** undergo changes. They have the same changes as in the *preterit* (or the past tense; see Chapter 6). These changes are as follows:

- ✔ **-car** verbs: **c → qu**
- ✔ **-gar** verbs: **g → gu**
- ✔ **-zar** verbs: **z → c**

The following table (and examples) show the full conjugation:

Infinitive	*Stem*	*Subjunctive Endings*
tocar *(to touch)*	**toqu-**	**-e, -es, -e, -emos, -éis, -en**
pagar *(to pay)*	**pagu-**	**-e, -es, -e, -emos, -éis, -en**
organizar *(to organize)*	**organic-**	**-e, -es, -e, -emos, éis, -en**

Here are some examples:

Es importante que no toques nada. *(It is important that you not touch anything.)*

Es imperativo que nosotros paguemos esta factura. *(It is imperative that we pay this bill.)*

Es necesario que él organice los datos. *(It is necessary for him to organize the data.)*

Coping with stem changes

Just like in the present tense, stem-changing **-ar** and **-er** verbs in the present subjunctive undergo changes in all forms except **nosotros** and **vosotros**. Table 8-7 outlines these changes.

Table 8-7	Verbs with Stem Changes in the Present Subjunctive			
Infinitive Ending	**Stem Change in the Present**	**Example Verb**	**yo, tú, él, ellos Subjunctive Stem**	**nosotros/ vosotros Subjunctive Stem**
-ar	e → ie	**cerrar** *(to close)*	cierr-	cerr-
-ar	o → ue	**mostrar** *(to show)*	muestr-	mostr-
-er	e → ie	**querer** *(to wish, to want)*	quier-	quer-
-er	o → ue	**volver** *(to return)*	vuelv-	volv-

Here are two example sentences with these verbs:

Quiero que Ud. cierre la ventana. *(I want you to close the window.)*

Es dudoso que ellos vuelvan temprano. *(It is doubtful that they will return early.)*

And what about **-ir** verbs? Well, **-ir** verbs with **e → ie** and **o → ue** stem changes make those same changes in all forms except

nosotros and **vosotros.** The **nosotros** and **vosotros** forms change **e** to **i** and **o** to **u,** respectively. Those with an **e** → **i** stem change use **i** instead of **e** in all forms including **nosotros** and **vosotros,** as shown in Table 8-8.

Table 8-8   Certain -ir Verbs with Present Subjunctive Stem Changes

Infinitive	Stem Change	Stem	nosotros and vosotros Stems
preferir *(to prefer)*	e → ie	prefier-	prefir-
dormir *(to sleep)*	o → ue	duerm-	durm-
servir *(to serve)*	e → i	sirv-	sirv-

Here are some examples of **-ir** verbs in the subjunctive:

> **La profesora está contenta que nosotros prefiramos ver una película española.** *(The teacher is happy that we prefer to see a Spanish film.)*

> **Su padre está enojado que él duerma hasta las diez.** *(His father is angry that he sleeps until ten o'clock.)*

> **Es dudoso que sirvan vino en la conferencia.** *(It is doubtful that they will serve wine at the conference.)*

The changes don't end with simple **-ar, -er,** and **-ir** verbs, however. Note the stem changes for the following categories of verbs that end with an additional vowel:

✓ Verbs that end in **-iar** have accent marks in all present subjunctive forms except **nosotros:**

   enviar *(to send):* envíe, envíes, envíe, enviemos, enviéis, envíen

✓ Verbs that end in **-uar** have accent marks in all present subjunctive forms except **nosotros:**

   continuar *(to continue):* continúe, continúes, continúe, continuemos, continuéis, continúen

✓ Verbs that end in **-uir** (but not **-guir**) add a **y** after the **u** in all present subjunctive forms:

   concluir *(to conclude):* concluya, concluyas, concluya, concluyamos, concluyáis, concluyan

The following examples show these rules in action:

Es importante que Ud. envíe este paquete inmediata-mente. *(It is important that you send this package immediately.)*

Me enfada que Ud. no continúe estudiando español. *(I'm annoyed that you don't continue to study Spanish.)*

El profesor desea que los estudiantes concluyan su trabajo. *(The teacher wants the students to complete their work.)*

Understanding verbs with both spelling and stem changes

Some very common Spanish verbs have both spelling and stem changes in the present subjunctive form, as shown in Table 8-9.

Table 8-9	Spelling and Stem Changes in the Present Subjunctive		
Verb	*Spelling Change*	*Stem Change*	*Subjunctive Forms*
colgar *(to hang)*	g → gu	o → ue	cuelgue, cuelgues, cuelgue, colguemos, colguéis, cuelguen
jugar *(to play)*	g → gu	u → ue	juegue, juegues, juegue, juguemos, juguéis, jueguen
comenzar *(to begin)*	z → c	e → ie	comience, comiences, comience, comencemos, comencéis, comiencen
empezar *(to begin)*	z → c	e → ie	empiece, empieces, empiece, empecemos, empecéis, empiecen
almorzar *(to eat lunch)*	z → c	o → ue	almuerce, almuerces, almuerce, almorcemos, almorcéis, almuercen

The following examples show these changes in action:

María está contenta de que sus perros jueguen en el jardín. *(María is happy that her dogs play in the backyard.)*

Estoy encantada que el espectáculo empiece ahora. *(I am delighted that the show will begin now.)*

La madre no permite que sus hijos almuercen en la sala. *(The mother doesn't permit her children to eat lunch in the living room.)*

Conjugating irregular verbs

Some verbs are completely irregular in the subjunctive mood, which means you can't follow any rules or patterns to form them. You can do nothing else but memorize them. Table 8-10 presents these verbs.

Table 8-10   Irregular Verbs in the Present Subjunctive

Spanish Verb	Subjunctive Forms
dar *(to give)*	**dé, des, dé, demos, deis, den**
estar *(to be)*	**esté, estés, esté, estemos, estéis, estén**
ir *(to go)*	**vaya, vayas, vaya, vayamos, vayáis, vayan**
saber *(to know)*	**sepa, sepas, sepa, sepamos, sepáis, sepan**
ser *(to be)*	**sea, seas, sea, seamos, seáis, sean**

Here are some examples of irregular verbs in the subjunctive:

Estamos tristes que tu abuela esté enferma. *(We are sad that your grandmother is sick.)*

Yo dudo que él sepa reparar la computadora. *(I doubt that he knows how to repair the computer.)*

Using the Present Subjunctive

The subjunctive mood is tentative and uncertain. It enables you to wish, desire, and suppose whenever reality falls short of expectations. It allows you to put all your shortcomings behind you and suppose, just for the time being, that you're something you're not or that certain conditions are in place that aren't really in place — "If only I were rich . . . ." The subjunctive also enables you to add a pinch of doubt to statements and offer impersonal opinions, so you can express yourself without being overly committal. It's an empowering grammatical construction.

The present subjunctive has many applications, which makes it a very useful tool for you to have. It allows you to express your innermost hopes, desires, and dreams; your most pressing needs; your wildest doubts; and your humblest opinions. Furthermore, it allows you to give advice, to insist on receiving what you want, to offer suggestions, and to demand the necessities of life. And you can execute these expressions in a very low-key, gentle way.

How do you know when to use the present subjunctive? You must use the subjunctive in Spanish (whether or not you'd use it in English) when all the following conditions exist within a sentence:

- ✔ The sentence contains a main (or *independent*) clause — a group of words containing a subject and a verb that can stand alone as a sentence — and a *subordinate* (or *dependent*) clause — a group of words containing a subject and a verb that can't stand alone. Generally, each clause must contain a different subject.

- ✔ The main clause shows, among other things, wishing, wanting, emotion, doubt, need, necessity, feelings, emotions, commands or orders, supposition, speculation, or opinion.

- ✔ **Que** *(that)* joins the main clause to the dependent clause, which contains a verb in the subjunctive.

When you use the subjunctive in English (and most people do so without even realizing it), you often omit the word *that*. In Spanish, however, you must always use **que** to join the two clauses:

Es improbable que yo salga esta noche. *(It is improbable [that] I'll go out tonight.)*

(No) Es extraño que él haga eso. *(It is [not] strange [that] he's doing that.)*

✔ The verb in the main clause is in the present, the future (see Chapter 7), or a command (see "Giving Commands with the Imperative Mood" earlier in this chapter).

Expressing your desires, needs, or doubts

One of the coolest features of the subjunctive mood is that it enables you to express desire, hope, or preference; offer suggestions, recommendations, or advice; and even insist or beg for what you want. In other words, even though you may not get what you want, you can certainly ask for it, hope for it, and even insist on it. These expressions of desire, hope, and preference require a combination of two clauses:

✔ The main clause expresses the desire, doubt, or opinion in the indicative mood (statement of fact): "I hope . . . ," "Sally advises . . . ," or "Pedro prefers . . ."

✔ The subordinate clause describes that which is being desired, doubted, or offered as an opinion, and you express it in the subjunctive mood. Using the first main clause (from the previous bullet) as an example: I hope "that my package arrives tomorrow."

The following list shows verbs that express wishing, emotion, need, doubt, advice, command, demand, desire, hope, permission, preference, prohibition, request, suggestion, or wanting and, therefore, require the use of the subjunctive in the subordinate clause. (Verbs with a * require a spelling or stem change; see the earlier "Forming the Present Subjunctive" section for more on making these changes.)

Spanish	*English*
aconsejar	*to advise*
alegrarse (de)	*to be glad, to be happy*
avergonzarse de	*to be ashamed of*
(no) creer	*to believe (disbelieve)*
desear	*to desire, to wish, to want*
dudar	*to doubt*
enfadarse	*to become angry*
enojarse	*to become angry*

Spanish	English
esperar	*to hope*
exigir*	*to require, to demand*
insistir	*to insist*
lamentar	*to regret*
mandar	*to command, to order*
necesitar	*to need*
negar*	*to deny*
ojalá (que) . . .	*if only . . .*
ordenar	*to order*
pedir*	*to ask for, to request*
permitir	*to permit*
preferir*	*to prefer*
prohibir	*to forbid*
querer*	*to wish, to want*
recomendar*	*to recommend*
requerir*	*to require*
rogar*	*to beg, to request*
sentir*	*to be sorry, to regret*
sugerir*	*to suggest*
suplicar	*to beg, to plead*
temer	*to fear*

Here's how you use some of these verbs:

Siento que Uds. no vengan a mi fiesta. *(I am sorry that you aren't coming to my party.)*

El patrón manda que Ud. llegue a tiempo. *(The boss demands that you arrive on time.)*

Ojalá que yo gane la loteria. *(If only I win the lottery.)*

If no doubt exists in the thought you want to express, you use the indicative (past, present, or future):

Él no duda que yo merezco el premio. *(He doesn't doubt that I deserve the award.)*

Yo creo que ella es muy inteligente. *(I believe she is very intelligent.)*

If the certainty is negated or questioned, however, you use the subjunctive:

> **¿No piensas que ese libro sea interesante?** *(Don't you think that book is interesting?)*

Demonstrating feelings or emotions

When the main clause of a Spanish sentence contains the word **estar** *(to be)* followed by an adjective that expresses feelings or emotions, you use the subjunctive in the dependent clause. To complete the sentence, you insert the words **de que** *(that)* after the adjective:

> **Estoy alegre de que Uds. me acompañen al cine.** *(I'm happy that you are accompanying me to the movies.)*

> **No estamos contentos de que tú pierdas el tiempo.** *(We are not happy that you are wasting time.)*

The following table lists many Spanish adjectives that express feelings or emotions (for more on adjectives, head to Chapter 4):

Spanish	*English*
alegre	*happy*
avergonzado (-a)	*embarrassed, ashamed*
contento (-a)	*happy*
encantado (-a)	*delighted*
enojado (-a)	*angry*
feliz	*happy*
furioso (-a)	*furious*
irritado (-a)	*irritated*
orgulloso (-a)	*proud*
triste	*sad*

You use the subjunctive after the adverbs **tal vez** *(perhaps)* and **quizás** *(perhaps)* to imply doubt or uncertainty. When you want to express certainty, you use the indicative:

> **Tal vez (Quizás) vayan a la América del Sur.** *(Perhaps they will go to South America.)*

Employing impersonal expressions

You use an impersonal expression to convey personal information and ideas without making any one person the owner. The impersonal expression acts as the main clause of the sentence and is joined to the thoughts you want to relate by **que** *(that)*. When this expression shows wishing, uncertainty, need, emotion, and so on, it requires the subjunctive in the dependent clause that follows.

Many (although not all) impersonal expressions begin with **es** *(it is)* and are followed by adjectives showing wishing, emotion, doubt, need, and so on. They require the subjunctive even if they're negated:

> **No es urgente que me telefonee.** *(It isn't urgent that you call me.)*

The following table lists some of the most common Spanish impersonal expressions that require the subjunctive:

Spanish	*English*
conviene que	*it is advisable that*
es absurdo que	*it is absurd that*
es asombroso que	*it is amazing that*
es bueno que	*it is good/nice that*
es conveniente que	*it is fitting that*
es curioso que	*it is curious that*
es difícil que	*it is difficult that*
es dudoso que	*it is doubtful that*
es esencial que	*it is essential that*
es extraño que	*it is strange that*
es fácil que	*it is easy that*
es importante que	*it is important that*
es imposible que	*it is impossible that*
es increíble que	*it is incredible that*
es injusto que	*it is unfair that*
es interesante que	*it is interesting that*
es irónico que	*it is ironic that*
es justo que	*it is fair that*
es lamentable que	*it is regrettable that*

Spanish	English
es malo que	it is bad that
es mejor que, más vale que	it is better that
es natural que	it is natural that
es necesario que, es preciso que	it is necessary that
es posible que	it is possible that
es preferible que	it is preferable that
es probable que	it is probable that
es raro que	it is rare that
es sorprendente que	it is surprising that
es suficiente que	it is enough that
es una lástima que	it is a pity that
es urgente que	it is urgent that
es útil que	it is useful that
parece mentira que	it seems untrue that

Here are some examples that show how an impersonal expression can communicate a very personal thought, feeling, or opinion:

> **Es sorprendente que esa mujer sea tan irresponsable.**
> *(It is surprising that that woman is so irresponsible.)*

> **Es injusto que estas personas no puedan votar.** *(It is unfair that these people can't vote.)*

Be careful! When impersonal expressions show certainty (such as the following), you must use the indicative (present, past, or future):

Spanish	English
es cierto	it is certain, it is sure
es claro	it is clear
es evidente	it is evident
es exacto	it is exact
es obvio	it is obvious
es seguro	it is sure
es verdad	it is true
parece	it seems

Es obvio que nuestros precios son competitivos. *(It is obvious that our prices are competitive.)*

Es claro que Ud. tiene razón. *(It is clear that you are right.)*

However, impersonal expressions that show certainty when used in the affirmative express doubt or denial when they're negated and, therefore, require the subjunctive:

Es cierto que el avión despega pronto. *(It is certain that the plane will take off soon.)*

No es cierto que el avión despegue pronto. *(It is uncertain that the plane will take off soon.)*

Using relative clauses

You use the subjunctive in *relative clauses,* where the person or thing mentioned in the main clause

- ✔ Is indefinite
- ✔ Is nonexistent
- ✔ Is sought after but not yet attained
- ✔ May or may not exist

In other words, the subject of the sentence just isn't sure or is in doubt about the availability of the person or thing. Here are two examples:

Busco un mecánico que sepa reparar mi coche. *(I am looking for a mechanic who knows how to repair my car.)*

Because of the indefinite quality of **mecánico,** you don't use the impersonal **a** here.

Conozco a un mecánico que sabe reparar mi coche. *(I know a mechanic who knows how to repair my car.)*

Note that in the first sentence, the subject is unsure if such a person can be found. In the second sentence, however, the subject has no doubt that the person exists, so the present tense, rather than the present subjunctive, is required.

Playing with the Present Perfect Subjunctive

You use the present perfect subjunctive when the verb in the main clause is in the present tense, and the dependent verb refers to an event that has taken place.

You form the present perfect subjunctive by conjugating the helping verb **haber** in the present subjunctive and adding the past participle of the main verb. (See Chapter 6.)

The following chart shows the verb **haber** conjugated in the present subjunctive:

haber [helping verb] *(to have)*	
haya	hayamos
hayas	hayáis
haya	hayan

Here's an example of how you combine a conjugation of **haber** with a past participle to form the present perfect subjunctive:

> **Espero que ellos hayan terminado su trabajo a tiempo.**
> *(I hope that they have finished their work on time.)*

Making Actions Conditional

Should've, could've, would've . . . that's what the conditional mood is all about. If the conditions were appropriate, the action should've, could've, or would've resulted . . . theoretically speaking. Simply put, you use the *conditional mood* to express a conditional action. But you can also use it to make a polite request or to subtly, or not so subtly, suggest that someone perform a certain action.

Forming the conditional of regular verbs

When conjugating Spanish verbs in the regular conditional mood, keep the following points in mind:

- ✔ The regular conditional mood is a combination of the future (see Chapter 7) and imperfect tenses (see Chapter 6).

- ✔ The regular conditional tense requires no spelling or stem changes.

When conjugating regular **-ar, -er,** and **-ir** verbs in the conditional tense, you simply take the entire verb infinitive (don't drop anything) and then add the imperfect verb endings you use for **-er** and **-ir** verbs: **-ía, -ías, ía, -íamos, -íais,** and **-ían,** as shown in the tables below:

preparar *(to prepare)*	
yo prepararía	nosotros prepararíamos
tú prepararías	vosotros prepararíais
él, ella, Ud. prepararía	ellos, ellas, Uds. prepararían
Ud. prepararía la comida. *(You* (formal) *would prepare the meal.)*	

vender *(to sell)*	
yo vendería	nosotros venderíamos
tú venderías	vosotros venderíais
él, ella, Ud. vendería	ellos, ellas, Uds. venderían
Vosotras venderíais el coche. *(You* (plural, female, familiar) *would sell the car)*	

escribir *(to write)*	
yo escribiría	nosotros escribiríamos
tú escribirías	vosotros escribiríais
él, ella, Ud. escribiría	ellos, ellas, Uds. escribirían
Ella escribiría la carta. *(She would write the letter.)*	

Here is an example of the conditional in use:

Yo no jugaría al golf. *(I wouldn't play golf.)*

Exploring verbs with irregular conditional forms

Certain Spanish verbs are irregular in the conditional. These verbs have irregular conditional stems, which always end in **-r** or **-rr** — an easy way to remember them! To form the conditional of these irregular verbs, you do one of three things:

✔ Drop **e** from the infinitive ending before adding the proper conditional ending:

Infinitive	*Conditional Stem*
caber *(to fit)*	cabr-
haber *(to have)*	habr-
poder *(to be able)*	podr-
querer *(to want)*	querr-
saber *(to know)*	sabr-

Here is an example sentence:

No querría verlo. *(I wouldn't want to see it.)*

✔ Drop **e** or **i** from the infinitive ending and replace the vowel with a **d** before adding the proper conditional ending:

Infinitive	*Conditional Stem*
poner *(to put)*	pondr-
salir *(to leave)*	saldr-
tener *(to have)*	tendr-
valer *(to be worth)*	valdr-
venir *(to come)*	vendr-

Here's a sentence illustrating the conditional:

Yo no pondría esos papeles en la mesa. *(I wouldn't put those papers on the table.)*

✔ Two high-frequency irregular verbs in the conditional are

Infinitive	Conditional Stem
decir *(to say)*	**dir-**
hacer *(to make, to do)*	**har-**

Observe these verbs in action:

Yo no diría eso. *(I wouldn't say that.)*

¿Qué harían para resolver el problema? *(What would they do to solve the problem?)*

Using the conditional

You use the conditional

✔ To express what would or could happen in the future:

Viajaría a España. *(I would travel to Spain.)*

✔ To make a polite request:

Me gustaría un helado. *(I would like an ice cream.)*

✔ To express wonderment or probability in the past:

¿Dónde estaría mi gato? *(I wonder where my cat was.)*

Estaría debajo de la mesa. *(It must have been under the table.)*

A sentence containing an *if clause* requires an advanced tense of the subjunctive that we don't discuss in this book.

Chapter 9

Ten Important Verb Distinctions

In This Chapter

▶ Avoiding verb mix-ups and selecting the proper verb

▶ Understanding different verb connotations

*J*ust like in English, you can describe actions or situations in Spanish by using different verbs, depending on the exact meaning you want to convey. In this chapter, we present ten pairs of Spanish verbs that are often misused because they have the same English meanings but different English connotations. We explain how you can determine which to use in any given situation.

Ser versus Estar

The verbs **ser** and **estar** always cause considerable confusion, because both verbs mean *to be*. You use each of these verbs differently, however.

You use **ser** to express the following:

▶ An inherent characteristic or quality (one that probably won't change any time soon):

  • **Mi abuela es vieja.** *(My grandmother is old.)*

▶ The identity of the subject:

  • **Mi padre es abogado.** *(My father is a lawyer.)*

✔ The date, time, or place of an event:

- **Es jueves.** *(It's Thursday.)*
- **Son las once.** *(It's eleven o'clock.)*
- **¿Dónde es el concierto?** *(Where is the concert?)*

✔ Origin and nationality:

- **Ella es de Cuba.** *(She is from Cuba.)*
- **Ella es cubana.** *(She is Cuban.)*

✔ Ownership:

- **Es mi perro.** *(It's my dog.)*

✔ Material:

- **Es de oro.** *(It's made of gold.)*

✔ An impersonal idea:

- **Es fácil escribir en español.** *(It's easy to write in Spanish.)*

On the other hand, you use **estar** to express

✔ Health:

¿Cómo estás? Estoy bien. *(How are you? I'm fine.)*

✔ Location, situation, or position:

El diccionario está en la mesa. *(The dictionary is on the table.)*

✔ Temporary conditions or states:

Ella está ocupada. *(She is busy.)*

✔ The progressive tense (see Chapter 3):

El niño está durmiendo. *(The child is sleeping.)*

Saber versus Conocer

Both **saber** and **conocer** mean *to know.* **Saber** expresses knowing how to do something or knowing a fact. **Conocer** expresses knowing in the sense of being acquainted with a person, place, thing, or idea. Note the differences in the following examples:

> **Yo sé hablar español.** *(I know how to speak Spanish.)*
>
> **Ella sabe mi nombre.** *(She knows my name.)*
>
> **Sabemos el poema.** *(We know the poem [by heart].)*
>
> **Yo conozco al señor López.** *(I know Mr. López.)*
>
> **¿Conoces este libro?** *(Do you know [Are you acquainted with] this book?)*
>
> **Conocemos el poema.** *(We know [are acquainted with] the poem.)*

Tomar versus Llevar

Determining the correct usage for **tomar** and **llevar** can be a bit tricky. Both verbs mean *to take*. You use **tomar** when the subject picks up something in his or her hands in order to physically carry it to another location. You use **llevar** when the subject is taking or leading a person/thing to a place or is carrying or transporting an item.

In most instances, if you can substitute the word "lead" or "carry" for "take," you should use the verb **llevar**. If you can't substitute one of those words, you should use **tomar.**

Here are some examples to help clarify:

> **Tomo tu lápiz.** *(I'm taking your pencil.)*
>
> **Tomó el niño de la mano.** *(He took the child by the hand.)*
>
> **Llevo a mi hermano a la playa.** *(I'm taking my brother to the beach.)*
>
> **Llevaron su coche al garaje.** *(They took their car to the garage.)*

You can compare the two verbs at work in this example sentence:

> **Tomé mi libro y lo llevé a la escuela.** *(I took my book and I brought it to school.)*

Deber versus Tener Que

You use both **deber** and **tener que** to express what a subject *must* or *has to* do. You generally use **deber** to express a moral obligation, whereas **tener que** expresses what has to be done:

> **Debes pedir permiso antes de salir.** *(You must ask for permission before going out.)*

> **Tengo que ir al dentista porque tengo un dolor de las muelas.** *(I have to go to the dentist because I have a toothache.)*

Preguntar versus Pedir

Preguntar and **pedir** both mean *to ask*. You use **preguntar** to show that the subject is asking a question or inquiring about someone or something. You use **pedir** to show that the subject is asking for or requesting something in particular:

> **Yo le pregunté por qué me pidió tu dirección.** *(I asked him why he asked me for your address.)*

Jugar versus Tocar

Jugar and **tocar** both mean *to play*. You use **jugar** when the subject is engaging in a sport or game. You use **tocar** when the subject is playing a musical instrument:

> **Ellos jugaban a los naipes mientras yo tocaba el piano.** *(They were playing cards while I was playing the piano.)*

Gastar versus Pasar

If you're into *spending*, **gastar** and **pasar** are the verbs you need. Those who love to spend money use **gastar**, but people who spend time engaging in an activity should use **pasar**:

> **Pasé dos semanas en México y gasté mucho dinero allí.** *(I spent two weeks in Mexico, and I spent a lot of money there.)*

Dejar versus Salir

Dejar expresses that the subject has left something behind, whereas **salir** expresses that the subject has left a place:

> **Voy a dejar mis gafas en casa.** *(I am going to leave my glasses at home.)*

> **Ella no puede salir sin ellos.** *(She can't leave without them.)*

Volver versus Devolver

Volver (ue) and **devolver (ue)** both have the same meaning — *to return* — and you conjugate them in the same way. Use **volver** when the subject is physically returning to a place. Use **devolver** when the subject is returning an item to its owner:

> **Siempre le devuelvo a ella sus llaves cuando vuelve a casa.** *(I always return her keys to her when she returns home.)*

Poder versus Saber

Poder and **saber** can be a tricky pair of verbs. Both verbs mean *can,* but here's how they differ: **Poder** shows that the subject has the ability to perform an action, and **saber** shows that the subject actually knows how to perform the action.

If you can substitute the words "knows how to" for "can," you should use **saber.** Otherwise, use **poder.** Here are some examples:

> **Yo puedo cocinar.** *(I can cook.)*

Here you're saying that you have the ability to cook, but that doesn't necessarily mean that you know *how* to cook.

> **Yo sé cocinar.** *(I can cook.)*

Now you're saying that, yes, you know how to cook!

Appendix

Verb Charts

• •

*T*his appendix is the place to look if you've forgotten a verb conjugation and don't have the patience to scan the table of contents and then search for the proper table in the book. Here you encounter verb charts that help you quickly find the conjugations for all the verbs you need in many Spanish tenses and moods.

Regular Verbs

The three families of Spanish verbs are those that end in **-ar, -er,** and **-ir.** Regular verbs within those categories follow the same rules for conjugation no matter the tense (present, past, or future) or mood (imperative or subjunctive). The regular verbs listed in this section drop their respective infinitive ending (**-ar, -er,** or **-ir**) and add the endings we have in bold.

-ar verbs

trabajar (to work)

Present participle: trabaj**ando**

Commands: ¡Trabaj**e** Ud.!, ¡Trabaj**en** Uds.!, ¡Trabaj**emos**!, ¡Trabaj**a** tú!, ¡No trabaj**es** tú!, ¡Trabaj**ad** vosotros!, ¡No trabaj**éis** vosotros!

Present: trabaj**o**, trabaj**as**, trabaj**a**, trabaj**amos**, trabaj**áis**, trabaj**an**

Preterit: trabaj**é**, trabaj**aste**, trabaj**ó**, trabaj**amos**, trabaj**asteis**, trabaj**aron**

Imperfect: trabaj**aba**, trabaj**abas**, trabaj**aba**, trabaj**ábamos**, trabaj**abais**, trabaj**aban**

Future: trabajar**é**, trabajar**ás**, trabajar**á**, trabajar**emos**, trabajar**éis**, trabajar**án**

Subjunctive: trabaj**e**, trabaj**es**, trabaj**e**, trabaj**emos**, trabaj**éis**, trabaj**en**

-er verbs

comer (to eat)

Present participle: com**iendo**

Commands: ¡Com**a** Ud.!, ¡Com**an** Uds.!, ¡Com**amos**!, ¡Com**e** tú!, ¡No com**as** tú!, ¡Com**ed** vosotros!, ¡No com**áis** vosotros!

Present: com**o**, com**es**, com**e**, com**emos**, com**éis**, com**en**

Preterit: com**í**, com**iste**, com**ió**, com**imos**, com**isteis**, com**ieron**

Imperfect: com**ía**, com**ías**, com**ía**, com**íamos**, com**íais**, com**ían**

Future: comer**é**, comer**ás**, comer**á**, comer**emos**, comer**éis**, comer**án**

Subjunctive: com**a**, com**as**, com**a**, com**amos**, com**áis**, com**an**

-ir verbs

abrir (to open)

Present participle: abr**iendo**

Commands: ¡Abr**a** Ud.!, ¡Abr**an** Uds.!, ¡Abr**amos**!, ¡Abr**e** tú!, ¡No abr**as** tú!, ¡Abr**id** vosotros!, No abr**áis** vosotros!

Present: abr**o**, abr**es**, abr**e**, abr**imos**, abr**ís**, abr**en**

Preterit: abr**í**, abr**iste**, abr**ió**, abr**imos**, abr**isteis**, abr**ieron**

Imperfect: abr**ía**, abr**ías**, abr**ía**, abr**íamos**, abr**íais**, abr**ían**

Future: abrir**é**, abrir**ás**, abrir**á**, abrir**emos**, abrir**éis**, abrir**án**

Subjunctive: abr**a**, abr**as**, abr**a**, abr**amos**, abr**áis**, abr**an**

Stem-Changing Verbs

Stem-changing verbs require an internal change in the *stem vowel* (the vowel before the **-ar, -er,** or **-ir** infinitive ending) in the **yo, tú, él, (ella, Ud.),** and **ellos (ellas, Uds.)** forms of certain tenses. We mark the stem changes in this section in bold. In all other tenses, stem-changing verbs don't require any change; they follow the examples given in the "Regular Verbs" section according to their infinitive ending.

-ar verbs

pensar (e to ie) (to think)

Present: p**ie**nso, p**ie**nsas, p**ie**nsa, pensamos, pensáis, p**ie**nsan

Subjunctive: p**ie**nse, p**ie**nses, p**ie**nse, pensemos, penséis, p**ie**nsen

Other verbs like **pensar** include **cerrar** *(to close),* **comenzar** *(to begin),* **despertarse** *(to wake up),* **empezar** *(to begin),* and **sentarse** *(to sit down).*

mostrar (o to ue) (to show)

Present: m**ue**stro, m**ue**stras, m**ue**stra, mostramos, mostráis, m**ue**stran

Subjunctive: m**ue**stre, m**ue**stres, m**ue**stre, mostremos, mostréis, m**ue**stren

Other verbs like **mostrar** include **acordarse de** *(to remember),* **almorzar** *(to eat lunch),* **acostarse** *(to go to bed),* **contar** *(to tell),* **costar** *(to cost),* **encontrar** *(to find),* **probar** *(to prove, to try),* and **recordar** *(to remember).*

jugar (u to ue) (to play [a sport or game])

Present: j**ue**go, j**ue**gas, j**ue**ga, jugamos, jugáis, j**ue**gan

Preterit: jugué, jugaste, jugó, jugamos, jugasteis, jugaron

Subjunctive: j**ue**gue, j**ue**gues, j**ue**gue, juguemos, juguéis, j**ue**guen

-er verbs

querer (e to ie) (to wish, want)

Present: quiero, quieres, quiere, queremos, queréis, quieren

Subjunctive: quiera, quieras, quiera, queramos, queráis, quieran

Other verbs like **querer** include **defender** *(to defend, to forbid)*, **descender** *(to descend)*, **entender** *(to understand, to hear)*, and **perder** *(to lose)*.

volver (o to ue) (to return)

Present: vuelvo, vuelves, vuelve, volvemos, volvéis, vuelven

Subjunctive: vuelva, vuelvas, vuelva, volvamos, volváis, vuelvan

Other verbs like **volver** include **devolver** *(to return)*, **envolver** *(to wrap)*, **llover** *(to rain)*, **morder** *(to bite)*, **mover** *(to move)*, and **poder** *(to be able to, can)*.

-ir verbs

pedir (e to i) (to ask)

Present participle: pidiendo

Present: pido, pides, pide, pedimos, pedís, piden

Preterit: pedí, pediste, pidió, pedimos, pedisteis, pidieron

Subjunctive: pida, pidas, pida, pidamos, pidáis, pidan

Other verbs like **pedir** include **impedir** *(to prevent)*, **medir** *(to measure)*, **repetir** *(to repeat)*, and **servir** *(to serve)*.

sentir (e to ie/i) (to feel)

Present participle: sintiendo

Present: siento, sientes, siente, sentimos, sentís, sienten

Preterit: sentí, sentiste, sintió, sentimos, sentisteis, sintieron

Subjunctive: sienta, sientas, sienta, sintamos, sintáis, sientan

Other verbs like **sentir** include **advertir** *(to warn, to notify)*, **consentir** *(to consent)*, **mentir** *(to lie)*, **preferir** *(to prefer)*, and **referir** *(to refer)*.

dormir (o to ue/u) (to sleep)

Present participle: durmiendo

Present: duermo, duermes, duerme, dormimos, dormís, duermen

Preterit: dormí, dormiste, durmió, dormimos, dormisteis, durmieron

Subjunctive: duerma, duermas, duerma, durmamos, durmáis, duerman

Another verb like **dormir** is **morir** *(to die)*.

-uir verbs (except -guir)

construir (add y) (to construct, build)

Present participle: construyendo

Present: construyo, construyes, construye, construimos, construís, construyen

Preterit: construí, construiste, construyó, construimos, construisteis, construyeron

Subjunctive: construya, construyas, construya, construyamos, construyáis, construyan

Other verbs like **construir** include **concluir** *(to conclude)*, **contribuir** *(to contribute)*, **destruir** *(to destroy)*, **incluir** *(to include)*, and **sustituir** *(to substitute)*.

-eer verbs

creer (add y) (to believe)

Preterit: creí, creíste, creyó, creímos, creísteis, creyeron

Other verbs like **creer** include **leer** *(to read)*, **poseer** *(to possess)*, and **proveer** *(to provide)*.

-iar verbs

guiar (i to í) (to guide)

> Present: guío, guías, guía, guiamos, guiáis, guían

> Subjunctive: guíe, guíes, guíe, guiemos, guiéis, guíen

Other verbs like **guiar** include **confiar** + **en** *(to confide in)*, **enviar** *(to send)*, **esquiar** *(to ski)*, and **variar** *(to vary)*.

-uar verbs

continuar (u to ú) (to continue)

> Present: continúo, continúas, continúa, continuamos, continuáis, continúan

> Subjunctive: continúe, continúes, continúe, continuemos, continuéis, continúen

Another verb like **continuar** is **actuar** *(to act)*.

Spelling-Change Verbs

Some verbs require a spelling change in certain tenses to preserve proper pronunciation. In all the tenses we don't list in this section, verbs with spelling changes don't require the changes; they follow the examples given in the "Regular Verbs" section according to their infinitive ending.

-car verbs

buscar (c to qu) (to look for)

> Preterit: bus**qu**é, buscaste, buscó, buscamos, buscasteis, buscaron

> Subjunctive: bus**qu**e, bus**qu**es, bus**qu**e, bus**qu**emos, bus**qu**éis, bus**qu**en

Other verbs like **buscar** include **acercar** *(to bring near)*, **aplicar** *(to apply)*, **criticar** *(to criticize)*, **educar** *(to educate)*, **explicar** *(to explain)*, **identificar** *(to identify)*, **pescar** *(to fish)*, **practicar** *(to practice)*, **sacar** *(to take out)*, and **significar** *(to mean)*.

-gar verbs

llegar (g to gu) (to arrive)

Preterit: lle**gu**é, llegaste, llegó, llegamos, llegasteis, llegaron

Subjunctive: lle**gue**, lle**gue**s, lle**gue**, lle**gue**mos, lle**gué**is, lle**gue**n

Other verbs like **llegar** include **apagar** (to extinguish), **castigar** (to punish), and **pagar** (to pay).

-zar verbs

lanzar (z to c) (to throw)

Preterit: lan**c**é, lanzaste, lanzó, lanzamos, lanzasteis, lanzaron

Subjunctive: lan**c**e, lan**c**es, lan**c**e, lan**c**emos, lan**c**éis, lan**c**en

Other verbs like **lanzar** include **avanzar** *(to advance),* **gozar** *(to enjoy),* **memorizar** *(to memorize),* **organizar** *(to organize),* and **utilizar** *(to use).*

Consonant + -cer or -cir verbs

ejercer (c to z) (to exercise)

Present: ejer**z**o, ejerces, ejerce, ejercemos, ejercéis, ejercen

Subjunctive: ejer**z**a, ejer**z**as, ejer**z**a, ejer**z**amos, ejer**z**áis, ejer**z**an

Other verbs like **ejercer** include **convencer** *(to convince)* and **vencer** *(to conquer).*

esparcir (c to z) (to spread out)

Present: espar**z**o, esparces, esparce, esparcimos, esparcís, esparcen

Subjunctive: espar**z**a, espar**z**as, espar**z**a, espar**z**amos, espar**z**áis, espar**z**an

Vowel + -cer or -cir verbs

conocer (c to zc) (to know)

Present: cono**z**co, conoces, conoce, conocemos, conocéis, conocen

Subjunctive: cono**z**ca, cono**z**cas, cono**z**ca, cono**z**camos, cono**z**cáis, cono**z**can

Other verbs like conocer include **crecer** *(to grow),* **desobedecer** *(to disobey),* **desaparacer** *(to disappear),* **establecer** *(to establish),* **obedecer** *(to obey),* **ofrecer** *(to offer),* and **parecer** *(to seem).*

traducir (c to zc) (to translate)

Present: tradu**z**co, traduces, traduce, traducimos, traducís, traducen

Subjunctive: tradu**z**ca, tradu**z**cas, tradu**z**ca, tradu**z**camos, tradu**z**cáis, tradu**z**can

Other verbs like **traducir** include **conducir** *(to drive),* **deducir** *(to deduce),* and **inducir** *(to induce).*

-ger or -gir verbs

escoger (g to j) (to choose)

Present: esco**j**o, escoges, escoge, escogemos, escogéis, escogen

Subjunctive: esco**j**a, esco**j**as, esco**j**a, esco**j**amos, esco**j**áis, esco**j**an

Other verbs like **escoger** include **coger** *(to take, to pick up),* **proteger** *(to protect),* and **recoger** *(to pick up).*

dirigir (g to j) (to direct)

Present: diri**j**o, diriges, dirige, dirigimos, dirigís, dirigen

Subjunctive: diri**j**a, diri**j**as, diri**j**a, diri**j**amos, diri**j**áis, diri**j**an

Another verb like **dirigir** is **exigir** *(to demand).*

-uir verbs

distinguir (gu to g) (to distinguish)

Present: distin**g**o, distingues, distingue, distinguimos, distinguís, distinguen

Subjunctive: distin**g**a, distin**g**as, distin**g**a, distin**g**amos, distin**g**áis, distin**g**an

Irregular Verbs

Irregular verbs may undergo changes in some or all tenses and moods and for some or all subjects. You must memorize the irregular forms (bolded here) because they follow no specific rules. For all the tenses we don't list in this section, the irregular verb follows the examples given in the "Regular Verbs" section according to its infinitive ending.

dar (to give)

Present: **doy,** das, da, damos, dais, dan

Preterit: **di, diste, dio, dimos, disteis, dieron**

Subjunctive: **dé,** des, **dé,** demos, deis, den

decir (to say, tell)

Present participle: **diciendo**

Affirmative Familiar Singular Command: **di**

Present: **digo, dices, dice,** decimos, decís, **dicen**

Preterit: **dije, dijiste, dijo, dijimos, dijisteis, dijeron**

Future: **diré, dirás, dirá, diremos, diréis, dirán**

Subjunctive: **diga, digas, diga, digamos, digáis, digan**

estar (to be)

Present: **estoy, estás, está,** estamos, estáis, **están**

Preterit: **estuve, estuviste, estuvo, estuvimos, estuvisteis, estuvieron**

Subjunctive: **esté, estés, esté,** estemos, estéis, **estén**

hacer (to make, do)

Affirmative Familiar Singular Command: **haz**

Present: **hago,** haces, hace, hacemos, hacéis, hacen

Preterit: **hice, hiciste, hizo, hicimos, hicisteis, hicieron**

Future: **haré, harás, hará, haremos, haréis, harán**

Subjunctive: **haga, hagas, haga, hagamos, hagáis, hagan**

ir (to go)

Present participle: **yendo**

Affirmative Familiar Command: **ve**

Present: **voy, vas, va, vamos, vais, van**

Preterit: **fui, fuiste, fue, fuimos, fuisteis, fueron**

Subjunctive: **vaya, vayas, vaya, vayamos, vayáis, vayan**

oír (to hear)

Present participle: **oyendo**

Affirmative Informal Singular Command: **oye**

Affirmative Informal Plural Command: **oíd**

Present: **oigo, oyes, oye,** oímos, oís, **oyen**

Preterit: **oí,** oíste, **oyó,** oímos, oísteis, **oyeron**

Subjunctive: **oiga, oigas, oiga, oigamos, oigáis, oigan**

poder (o to ue) (to be able to, can)

Present participle: **pudiendo**

Present: **puedo, puedes, puede,** podemos, podéis, **pueden**

Preterit: **pude, pudiste, pudo, pudimos, pudisteis, pudieron**

Future: **podré, podrás, podrá, podremos, podréis, podrán**

Subjunctive: **pueda, puedas, pueda,** podamos, podáis, **puedan**

poner (to put)

Past participle: **puesto**

Affirmative Familiar Singular Command: **pon**

Present: **pongo,** pones, pone, ponemos, ponéis, ponen

Preterit: **puse, pusiste, puso, pusimos, pusisteis, pusieron**

Future: **pondré, pondrás, pondrá, pondremos, pondréis, pondrán**

Subjunctive: **ponga, pongas, ponga, pongamos, pongáis, pongan**

querer (to want, wish)

Present: **quiero, quieres, quiere,** queremos, **queréis, quieren**

Preterit: **quise, quisiste, quiso, quisimos, quisisteis, quisieron**

Future: **querré, querrás, querrá, querremos, querréis, querrán**

Subjunctive: **quiera, quieras, quiera,** queramos, queráis, **quieran**

saber (to know)

Present: **sé,** sabes, sabe, sabemos, sabéis, saben

Preterit: **supe, supiste, supo, supimos, supisteis, supieron**

Future: **sabré, sabrás, sabrá, sabremos, sabréis, sabrán**

Subjunctive: **sepa, sepas, sepa, sepamos, sepáis, sepan**

salir (to go out, leave)

Affirmative Familiar Singular Command: **sal**

Present: **salgo,** sales, sale, salimos, salís, salen

Future: **saldré, saldrás, saldrá, saldremos, saldréis, saldrán**

Subjunctive: **salga, salgas, salga, salgamos, salgáis, salgan**

ser (to be)

Affirmative Familiar Singular Command: **sé**

Present: **soy, eres, es, somos, sois, son**

Preterit: **fui, fuiste, fue, fuimos, fuisteis, fueron**

Imperfect: **era, eras, era, éramos, erais, eran**

Subjunctive: **sea, seas, sea, seamos, seáis, sean**

tener (to have)

Affirmative Familiar Singular Command: **ten**

Present: **tengo, tienes, tiene,** tenemos, **tenéis, tienen**

Preterit: **tuve, tuviste, tuvo, tuvimos, tuvisteis, tuvieron**

Future: **tendré, tendrás, tendrá, tendremos, tendréis, tendrán**

Subjunctive: **tenga, tengas, tenga, tengamos, tengáis, tengan**

traer (to bring)

Present: **traigo,** traes, trae, traemos, traéis, traen

Preterit: **traje, trajiste, trajo, trajimos, trajisteis, trajeron**

Subjunctive: **traiga, traigas, traiga, traigamos, traigáis, traigan**

venir (to come)

Present participle: **viniendo**

Affirmative Familiar Singular Command: **ven**

Present: **vengo, vienes, viene,** venimos, **venís, vienen**

Preterit: **vine, viniste, vino, vinimos, vinisteis, vinieron**

Future: **vendré, vendrás, vendrá, vendremos, vendréis, vendrán**

Subjunctive: **venga, vengas, venga, vengamos, vengáis, vengan**

ver (to see)

Present: **veo,** ves, ve, vemos, veis, ven

Preterit: **vi,** viste, **vio,** vimos, visteis, vieron

Imperfect: **veía, veías, veía, veíamos, veíais, veían**

Subjunctive: **vea, veas, vea, veamos, veáis, vean**

Index